D0971137

Nobody Knows Anything

Investing Basics

Learn to Ignore the Experts, the Gurus and other Fools

Robert Moriarty

Also by Robert Moriarty
   The Art of Peace
   Crap Shoot
   Exposed!
   Entrapped!

Second Edition

Typesetting and layout work by Jeremy Irwin, jc9cz@yahoo.com

Thanks to Clive Maund for help with the charts

Library of Congress Cataloging-in-Publication Data has been applied for.

ISBN: 978-1533087140

Dedication

To Barbara, my companion, my love, my best friend and source of my endless sense of wonder at how remarkable she is.

"Nobody knows anything ... Not one person in the entire motion picture field knows for a certainty what's going to work. Every time out it's a guess and, if you're lucky, an educated one."

— William Goldman, *Adventures in the Screen Trade*

"The fool doth think he is wise, but the wise man knows himself to be a fool."

— William Shakespeare, *As You Like It*

"Men, it has been well said, think in herds; it will be seen that they go mad in herds, while they only recover their senses slowly, and one by one."

— Charles Mackay, *Memoirs of Extraordinary Popular Delusions and the Madness of Crowds*

"I can calculate the movement of stars, but not the madness of men."

— Attributed to Isaac Newton after he lost his life savings in the South Sea Bubble, 1720

"Leave them; they are blind guides of the blind. If a blind man leads a blind man, both will fall into a pit."

— Matthew 15:13-14

"Beware of false prophets, who come to you in sheep's clothing, but inwardly they are ravenous wolves. You will know them by their fruit."

— Matthew 7:15-16

"Bull markets are born on pessimism, grown on skepticism, mature on optimism, and die on euphoria. The time of maximum pessimism is the best time to buy, and the time of maximum optimism is the best time to sell."

— John Templeton, legendary investor

"For it is dangerous to attach one's self to the crowd in front, and so long as each one of us is more willing to trust another than to judge for himself, we never show any judgment in the matter of living, but always a blind trust, and a mistake that has been passed on from hand to hand finally involves us and works our destruction.

"It is the example of other people that is our undoing; let us merely separate ourselves from the crowd, and we shall be made whole. But as it is, the populace, defending its own iniquity, pits itself against reason."

— Seneca

"Many have made a trade of delusions and false miracles, deceiving the stupid multitudes."

— Leonardo da Vinci

CONTENTS

Introduction

WITH TENS OF THOUSANDS of books in print on the subject of investing, it would appear at first glance that making a profitable investment would be as simple as putting your chips down on a craps table and throwing the dice, only to collect your winnings a few moments later. But if it were quite that simple, why would we need tens of thousands of books packed with confusing and often conflicting information? Still we remain poor.

I was chatting with a friend of mine about investing, trying to make the point that we make things way too complicated. It's easier to profit if we skip a lot of the nonsense associated with investing and go directly to the core. Investing for profit isn't as difficult as the so-called gurus would have us believe, but like a contractor building a house, we have to start with a proper foundation.

I've run a successful financial website for fifteen years at 321gold.com. It started out as a way to pass on information about concepts and companies I was familiar with to friends and family, and it grew. And grew. From the beginning I was determined to cut out as much as possible of the voodoo and hocus pocus from the pieces we published, so we could attract serious investors.

So you will never read about the New World

Order or aliens or manipulation or conspiracies on my site. They may all be perfectly true but at the same time they are perfectly meaningless. You can't profit by betting on aliens or manipulation, so why bother worrying about them? One of the most basic bits of investment advice I would give any investor would be to learn the difference between signal and noise. Most investors and all unsuccessful investors focus on noise and ignore signal.

We've posted the work of somewhere between three hundred and four hundred writers on our site, and have linked to the work of thousands more. If we have misplaced a really great writer somewhere along the way, write me and let me know. We are always looking to expand the information we post.

As I was saying to my friend, some of the most basic bits of background in investing are missing from most investment books. The authors tend to write about their personal agendas without ever providing some of the most essential building blocks that every investor needs to know.

If you are going to be a successful carpenter, someone needs to teach you how to buy and hold a hammer in the correct way so your nails go in straight. If you are going to be a successful investor you need to know some of the basics about investments that are rarely found in books. We learn them through trial and error, and that makes for both bad carpentry and poor investing.

I've made money and I've lost money. I have made some brilliant and timely calls, and I've made enough boneheaded calls, and in public, that it's obvious I'm not a crook or a shill.

This book will not make you rich but it may keep you from being poor. It has been written with the benefit of almost fifty years' experience around financial markets. Since my website tends to specialize in finance and resources, many of the analogies and stories I tell here are around the subjects of gold and silver. But you don't have to own gold to get rich, as long as you aren't buying into the housing market or stock market at the very top.

I have had the marvelous opportunity to meet and talk with most of the great writers and thinkers about matters financial over the past fifteen years. I don't agree 100 per cent with any of them, including myself. I reserve the right to change my point of view in an instant.

Since my website did not ever rely on subscriptions, we weren't forced into the fatal position of having to tell the punters what they want to hear, in the way that most subscription sites are forced to.

Running a financial site is no more difficult than becoming a successful politician; all you have to do is tell people what they want to hear. We wouldn't dream of voting for a politician who told the truth, so why would we pay money to a website that was brutally honest with us? After all, we all have fantasies that we want fulfilled.

My wife and I had previously run an early and successful Macintosh computer upgrade website. We were experienced in the ways of getting people to visit a site and we knew how to sell products on it. With hundreds of tiny Canadian juniors needing someone to tell their stories, we determined that we would forgo the subscription model and make our income from advertising junior mining companies.

We had a few giant successes such as NovaGold, Silver Standard, and Sterling Mining. Eventually the quality of management or lack of talent took the companies in whatever direction they were determined to go. I soon learned that if the management of a company is dumb enough, they could always snatch defeat out of the jaws of victory.

My website was designed from the gitgo to make investors think. If I haven't pissed off every investor or reader at one point in time or another, I apologize. I'm trying to get readers to think, and if you are reading only what you agree with, you will soon be poor. None of us has all the answers and if you don't question your beliefs regularly you will never get it right in life.

Chapter 1
Nobody Knows Anything

INVESTORS HAVE COME TO BELIEVE that they need to find a guru, a financial advisor, or to read articles about certain theories of investing if they are to become rich from their investments. Those notions are all wrong. There are no gurus. Financial advisors advise because they have to earn a living. If they were experts on investing, they wouldn't need to be selling their services. The different theories about investing mostly remain interesting theories.

If you have good sense, keep an open mind and learn the basics, you don't need all the fluff. In short, there are no experts. Nobody knows anything.

Learn to think for yourself. If you can actually understand both people and how markets really work, it's possible to invest wisely. If you don't understand the behavior of people or how markets work, good luck with that.

If you read only one investment book in your entire life, don't make it *this* book. Make it the classic book on human behavior first published in 1841 called *Memoirs of Extraordinary Popular Delusions and the Madness of Crowds*, by Charles Mackay. I'll call it *EPD* from here on out, otherwise I'd spend the rest of my time typing. You can find and download the Kindle version on Amazon for free or you can pay a few dollars for a paper copy.

Most successful investors find *EPD* to be the most valuable insight into how humans act and react they will ever read.

I'll make one absolute demand right now. Buy or download *EPD* and read it. If you aren't willing to do that, you will never, never, ever make money. Stack your $100 bills up in a giant pile in your front yard and burn them along with this book.

If you aren't willing to invest or capable of investing enough time to read a single book, you will never become a successful investor.

Investing is like everything else you will ever do in life. If you don't invest of yourself, there will be no return because you will not value your knowledge. Think of it as homework for the soul, with the soul in this case being the soul of investing.

After I left the military service in 1970 I began to go to college, which my parents had insisted was necessary if I were ever to land a good job and become successful. It was as much bullshit as most of the things I heard from adults when I was a child, but that makes for another book in itself.

The second college that I attended, out of the five that I tried, was Southern Methodist University in Dallas. While SMU was well known (and accurately so) as being a party school for kids whose parents had more dollars than sense, it had a basic core curriculum that was actually quite good.

We were required to take a course on comparative religion. That could be handy in life. I've listened ad nauseam to the verbosity of religious converts who could extol at length on why their God was so wonderful and how every other religion was made up of heathens better suited for pitchforks and the fire, when I realized after a few minutes that they had no idea of what any other religion stood for. Most religious people find it remarkably easy to hate, although hatred is the basis of no religions.

SMU made every freshman take a course on drugs and alcohol. Now that was handy. I can assure you there was a lot of homework being done back in the dorms in 1971, as well as the study of comparative anatomy.

One required course was to read *EPD* in its entirety and write an essay. One book, one course, for one semester, three credit hours.

I'm a speed-reader. My mother gave the gift of a love of reading to my twin brother and me before we went to kindergarten. I never learned to read the way kids have been taught for the past 100 years in school so I never learned the bad habits, such as mouthing the words.

I can read 1,500 words a minute. It drives Barbara crazy since she believes if you flip pages every few seconds because you are reading so fast, you cannot comprehend. Take my word, you can. I devour books, often one a day. That's after a few hours on the computer reading a hundred articles to determine which few are worth sharing with our readers.

I loved reading *EPD*. The first few chapters were about investment bubbles, including the Mississippi Company bubble of 1718-1720 engineered by John Law, the South Sea Bubble of 1720 which proved the British investor was just as capable of mass stupidity as his French counterpart, and the tulip bulb craze in Holland from 1637. In fact if you are aware of the tulip bulb craze, the source of your information would have originally been *EPD*.

If all you read of the book is the first three chapters on past financial bubbles, you will have gained some insight into irrational investing. But continue reading.

After the few chapters on financial stupidity in history Mackay attacks even more interesting subjects such as alchemy, and how some of the learned men of science spent much of their lives in the search for the philosopher's stone reputed to be able to turn base metals into much sought after gold. He looked at the search for a universal cure for all diseases as a way of infinitely prolonging life.

The alchemists of course never succeeded. Even if they had, it would have been for nothing. Gold gains value only because it's rare. If gold suddenly became as ordinary as lead it would lose its value altogether. However, you could make some really cool looking bullets to put into your holster.

EPD continues at length, with tale after tale of various scoundrels and con men, and what seemed most interesting to me was the length of time for which they got away with their scams.

One, a certain Count St. Germain, claimed to have made his fortune first discovering and then peddling an elixir of life to people in Germany. He became the toast of Paris, where he convinced the Parisians that he was over 2,000 years old and had walked the shores of Galilee and attended the wedding party where Jesus turned water into wine. When telling people what they want to hear, it always helps to speak with great conviction.

The count even enlisted the aid of his servant when necessary. Once, at a party in Paris and surrounded by skeptics, he turned to his servant and asked if what he said was true. Without skipping a beat the servant replied, "I really cannot say. You forget, sir, I have only been five hundred years in your service."

His master replied, "I remember now; it was a little before your time!"

Predictions of the end of the world were always popular, as those who remember all the forecasts of calamity coming due in the year 2000 will cheerfully attest. Starting about the year 950, religious fanatics from France, Germany, even Italy began to proclaim the pending end of the world and the last judgment that would soon take place in Jerusalem.

By the middle of the year 999, so many pilgrims were converging on the Middle East that they had taken on the appearance of an army. To quote Mackay, "Knights, citizens, and serfs, travelled eastwards in company, taking with them their wives and children, singing psalms as they went, and looking with fearful eyes upon the sky, which they expected each minute to open, to let the Son of God descend in his glory."

But the world didn't end, much to the disappointment of the mob who were looking for a little more excitement in their lives.

By 1761 two minor earthquakes had struck near London, alarming the locals who proved all too willing to believe the prophecy of a third and even more deadly quake from a shell-shocked military veteran who proclaimed London would be destroyed entirely on the fifth of April that year. The earthquake didn't get the word and never happened. London was saved and the nutcase got locked up in the loony bin.

Then we had the case of the magic chicken in Leeds in 1806 that laid eggs inscribed with the words, "Christ is coming." Promptly a religious conversion took place among citizens from far and wide traveling to see the magic eggs. Convinced of an impending Day of Judgment, the believers prayed with great violence and swore to never sin again. Eventually someone realized the eggs had been inscribed upon with corrosive ink and then forced back into the poor innocent chicken, only to plop out again eventually.

Predictions of calamity were always popular. One called for the devil to poison all of Milan in the year 1630. By chance the bubonic plague did show up and killed much of the population. The now hysterical citizens ran to and fro throughout the city, looking for people to blame. An old man, older than eighty, raised the skirt of his cloak to wipe the stool upon which he was about to sit on, in a church. A mob of old women grabbed him and yanked him by the hair and started dragging him to a local magistrate, so that he could be put upon the rack to determine the truth of his evilness. Alas, he perished while being pulled through the streets.

Another man, a chemist and barber, stood accused of being in league with the devil in his nefarious plans. Being caught with various preparations, for after all he was a chemist, he was placed on the rack to determine the truth. He held out his innocence for the longest time until, finally realizing that admitting guilt would end the torture a long time before claims of innocence would, he confessed, as those being racked so often do. As a gesture of goodwill towards his torturers, he admitted several of his acquaintances as being part of the fictional alliance with the devil. They were promptly put to the rack and to no one's surprise they confessed as well, before all being executed.

It didn't take much to cause panic among a

population. Earthquakes, comets, and the latest attack of the plague could always bring out a flurry of astrologers and fortune-tellers to explain away the latest causes of doom. This could be why gurus remain so popular even today. When their predictions never quite come to fruition, the masses of people caught up in the nonsense have someone else to blame. After all, it's not their stupidity as individuals; it's all the fault of the guru.

An eyewitness to the Great Fire of London in September of 1666 reported that a certain Mother Shipton had made a prediction that London would be destroyed in its entirety by fire. When a small fire actually started in a bakery in Pudding Lane, the citizens of London stood by and watched as the self-fulfilling prophecy came true.

But if you think about it for a moment, predicting a fire in a town crammed with houses and shops made of wood isn't exactly brain surgery or rocket science. And if you can convince the locals to sit around and roast marshmallows instead of fighting the fire, a disaster is bound to occur.

Mackay relays the tale of prophets who failed to be honored in their time. One Peter of Pontefract predicted the death of King John before Ascension Day in 1213. The prediction pissed off the king, who promptly tossed poor Peter into the slammer until Ascension Day passed, and then hanged prophet Peter and his son for good riddance.

Other prophets were held in great esteem during their lifetimes and indeed still remain popular. The best known is perhaps Nostradamus, who produced upwards of one thousand couplets, each as obscure as the rest. Mackay uses the example of Nostradamus' second-century prediction 66, where he said:

From great dangers the captive is escaped.
A little time, great fortune changed.
In the palace the people are caught.
By good augury the city is besieged.

Those who choose to believe in the power of prediction claim that the stanza clearly refers to the imprisonment of Napoleon on Elba, his escape, his changed fortune, and the occupation of Paris by the enemies of France in turn.

But think about it for just a moment, and about the entire purpose of my demanding you read *EPD*. Captives escape all the time, great fortunes do change, people are caught in palaces and cities remain besieged on a regular basis.

Way before today's modern science of Technical Analysis, Mackay talks of such pseudo sciences as geomancy, whereby practitioners could foretell the future by means of lines and circles. Is there any real difference between the two?

My favorite form of predicting the future would have to be augury, whereby the "expert" could predict

13

events by means of reading either the flight or the entrails of birds, including chickens. And of course you have to consider divination, by which you could foresee events by careful study of tealeaves or cards or by reading the lines on people's hands.

Mackay doesn't skip on the art of interpreting dreams or the study of omens or any other mass superstition, such as the healing properties of magnets. Astrology is covered as it was as popular 170 years ago as it remains today.

EPD even went into the influence of politics and religion on the length of men's hair. It seems Alexander the Great believed beards on soldiers to be a weak point, as it was possible for the enemy to grab the beards of his men as a convenient handle prior to chopping off their heads. So he insisted his army remain clean-shaven.

On the other hand, it seems North American Indians believed in the art of chivalry. They insisted that warriors keep one long lock of hair on the top of the head so that their enemies had something to hold on to when they wanted to scalp them. It was a point of honor among the Indians to make it easier for the enemy to scalp them.

At the end of the eleventh century, the Pope and his minions made it clear that those men who wore long hair were automatically excommunicated. During the reign of Henry I of England, his own chaplain preached a sermon to the entire court based on the writing of St. Paul, in which he made it clear that terrible things would happen should the court keep their long ringlets.

Several of the king's men were so terrified that they broke into tears at the thought of eternal damnation because of the length of their hair. Even the king was observed to weep. The priest promptly pulled out his scissors and chopped the king's hair short. Within a few months the court forgot about the promise of eternal damnation and let their tresses return.

Across the pond in France, the French king, Louis VII, proved more obedient to the Pope. He kept his hair cut as short as the clergy. His queen, the vibrant and young Eleanor of Guienne, prior to her marriage to Louis at the age of fifteen, was considered the most eligible female in Europe. She hated his trim cut and left him when she was thirty.

She found the longer tresses of Henry, Duke of Normandy, more to her taste and promptly married him. She went on to spawn another eight children with him. He went on to become King Henry II of England.

Since her first marriage had ended not in a divorce but an annulment, her dowry of land was returned to her. She retained the incredibly valuable Duchy of Aquitaine after her marriage to Henry II and it became part of England. That footing of England within France led to centuries of bloody wars between the two countries. All because of a bad hair day.

England once found itself divided into two great parties based on the length of one's hair. The Cavaliers let their hair grow long, the Roundheads showed their great piety with their lack of locks. Each despised the other and demonstrated their beliefs with their length of hair.

Under the rule of Peter the Great of Russia, from 1682 to 1725, all males were required to either shave their beards or pay a tax of 100 roubles, a not inconsiderable sum at the time. Priests and serfs might be allowed to retain their beards but must pay one kopeck each time they passed the gate of a city. The citizens showed great discontent but as Charles Mackay puts it, "thousands who had the will had not the courage to revolt."

Those who didn't pay the tax and couldn't produce a receipt were promptly thrown into prison. For many years the tax collectors in Russia made a healthy sum from this source.

When writing about mass delusions and the madness of crowds, what would a book be without a serious discussion of religion? Nothing in the known universe approaches the delusional behavior of humans when engaged in the practice of religion, except perhaps investors in silver.

Pilgrims from Europe made regular pilgrimages to the Holy Land as early as the eighth, ninth and tenth centuries. Naturally the traveling was dangerous, with brigands showing up at every corner eager to relieve the tourists of their every dime. And nothing has changed today; it's exactly the same.

The pious visited Palestine in the hope their pilgrimage might "rub off the long score of sins, however atrocious." Every year the number of travelers increased. Everything they saw and held had great value to them. Eager salesmen provided wood guaranteed to be from the true cross, tears from the Virgin Mary, even tents that Paul had made ten centuries before.

The pilgrims were treated with the greatest respect and courtesy by the rulers of Syria through whose territory they had to pass, even if they did levy a tax on each of the pious intent on entering Jerusalem.

As the eleventh century approached a mass hysteria began and "the weak, the credulous, and the guilty, who in those days formed more than nineteen-twentieths of the population" believed the second coming of Christ was approaching, and they intended to relieve themselves of their sins through the long and dangerous pilgrimage.

Every possible sign — hurricanes, storms, earth-quakes, even shooting stars — seemed to tell a tale of impending doom and approaching judgment. The mass army of sinners hoping to be saved approached Jerusalem only to find that a new and less benevolent ruler had taken over. The Turks were now in charge of the Holy Land and they proved more ferocious and far less scrupulous than the Syrians of yore.

They also didn't approve of the mass of pilgrims overrunning the country and who seemingly had no intention of leaving for their own homeland, as the visitors had done for hundreds of years. "They were plundered and beaten with stripes, and kept in suspense for months at the gates of Jerusalem, unable to pay the golden bezant that was to procure them admission."

When it proved that the Day of Judgment wasn't quite at hand, as the pilgrims had believed, a few of the pious returned to Europe filled with indignation at the treatment they had received. The worse the tales of woe and the greater the dangers of the travel, the greater were the number of new hordes from Europe who insisted on making the same journey.

The Middle East had the wood, it had the kerosene, and all it needed was a tiny spark. That appeared in the form of a monk with the name of Peter the Hermit. As described by Mackay, he was "Enthusiastic, chivalrous, bigoted, and, if not insane, not far removed from insanity, he was the very prototype of the time. True enthusiasm is always persevering and always eloquent, and these two qualities were united in no common degree in the person of this extraordinary preacher."

While the serfs had no rights in this world, according to the clergy, the church convinced them they would have all the rights in the next. The concept of voting didn't exist. The peasants did what they were told and the churches told them they needed to go start a crusade and free the Holy Land.

Peter the Hermit came up with the idea of a crusade while still in Jerusalem after meeting with Simeon, the patriarch of the Greek Church in Palestine. This pair agreed the Turks had abused Christians and it was only right for all of Christendom to rise up and smite the heathen.

Peter returned to Italy to meet with Pope Urban II. Soon the Pope was equally enthusiastic about the idea of freeing Palestine from the Turks. The Pope gave Peter his papal blessing and sent him all over Europe to plead for a holy war. Tens of thousands answered his call.

The Pope in turn called for a council to consider the state of the church and to prepare for war in 1095. The seven-day meeting took place at Clermont, in Auvergne. At its conclusion the Pope, surrounded by all his cardinals and bishops decked out in all their glory, made a stirring speech encouraging the masses to prepare for war.

> *"I call upon you to wipe off these impurities from the face of the earth, and lift your oppressed fellow Christians from the depths into which they have been trampled. The sepulcher of Christ is possessed by the heathen, the sacred places dishonored by their vileness. Oh, brave knights*

and faithful people! Offspring of invincible fathers! Ye will not degenerate from your ancient renown. Ye will not be restrained from embarking in this great cause by tender ties of wife or little ones, but will remember the words of the Savior of the world himself, 'Whosoever loves father and mother more than me is not worthy of me. Whosoever shall abandon for my name's sake his house, or his brethren, or his sisters, or his father, or his mother, or his wife, or his children, or his lands, shall receive a hundredfold, and shall inherit eternal life.'"

That promise of eternal life always seems to be a deal maker, if the hundredfold return isn't enough. Tens of thousands more enlisted for the First Crusade. They were at best an ignorant rabble ill-prepared for any conflict. Peter's horde began to practice their warfare in Germany, against Jews, presuming that killing one heathen was just as good as killing another. The Jews weren't thrilled.

The concept of having all your sins forgiven simply by signing up for a war in some far off "Holy Land" proved popular, since the serfs of the time seem to have done a lot of sinning. Presumably you would be forgiven for any sins you continued to commit, so the Crusaders always were a mass of criminal thugs no matter where they went.

The horde was greeted at first with some degree

of kindness as they passed into Hungary on their way to the Middle East. Christians in Hungary weren't as enthusiastic about the idea of a Crusade as those from western Europe, but they weren't against it. At least, not until the mob began attacking and plundering the local communities. The Crusaders literally swarmed over the countryside, looting and murdering.

Eventually the Hungarians gathered together in larger numbers and began to attack the rear of the mass of Crusaders. Entering Bulgaria, the throng was greeted no better. Cities refused to supply them with provisions and the country people massacred the followers. By the time the group made it as far as Constantinople, the mass of unwashed and ill-mannered oafs had shrunk by two-thirds.

Peter's horde soon made themselves just as unpopular in Constantinople as they had in Germany, Hungary and Bulgaria. The mob set fire to several public buildings in the city out of pure spite and went so far as to strip the lead off the roofs of the churches, which they promptly sold to scrap metal dealers.

That pissed off the Emperor Alexius, ruler of Constantinople, and tainted all his actions not only towards the horde of Peter the Hermit but also to those more restrained armies that followed in the months passing. He seemed to feel that any mob of pilgrims was more of an enemy than the Turks were.

He sent them on their way to Asia Minor, where the Turks promptly slaughtered the untrained and poorly led rabble. In one of the first major battles, among a force of twenty-five thousand Christians some twenty-two thousand died. The Emperor saved the remaining three thousand from sure slaughter and paid a small sum to each of the survivors as a one-way ticket back to their homes in Europe.

As these events transpired, even more ill-trained and ill-led troops swarmed through Germany, Hungary and Bulgaria like a plague of locusts, determined to consume everything in their path. The King of Hungary determined that only extermination would do, and he had his men slaughter the pilgrims in great numbers. Other groups following proved even more determined to rape, loot and plunder. These hordes killed all the Jews they could lay their hands on after first subjecting them to the most terrible torture.

Once more passing through Hungary, so many of the faithful fanatics were slaughtered due to their looting and murdering that "fields were actually heaped with their corpses, and that for miles in its course the waters of the Danube were dyed with their blood."

The various armies of Crusaders made it as far as Constantinople before moving on to the Holy Land. Emperor Alexius labored under the mistaken belief that the Crusaders were operating on his behalf, but they pretty much went where they wanted and did what they wished. As mobs go, they were an especially unruly mass.

More battles commenced and the Turks began to lose as the military prowess of the Crusaders improved with time and experience. In 1099 Crusader forces managed to capture Jerusalem and kill thousands of innocent women and children in what would become a common practice with Crusaders over the decades.

One Crusade followed another and another. Eventually there were a total of eight major Crusades, each consisting of a lot of rape, looting and plundering, and a number of minor military operations that came under the umbrella of a Crusade. The deterioration of relations with their erstwhile allies in the Byzantine Empire led to the sack of Constantinople during the Third Crusade in 1204.

The art and practice of killing enemies of the Christian faith continued to grow, with some of the Crusades being no more than the rooting out of anyone who dared question the church. The Albigensian Crusade from 1208 to 1229 went after the heretical Cathars or Albigensian sect of Christianity in France. The Baltic Crusades from 1211 to 1225 went after pagans in Transylvania.

During those days, you could not only get killed for believing in a different god, you could die for just having a slightly different interpretation of a similar religion. Nothing has changed today.

In conclusion, Mackay goes on, "Now what was the grand result of all these struggles? Europe expended millions of her treasures, and the blood of two million of her children; and a handful of quarrelsome knights retained possession of Palestine for about one hundred years!"

The Crusades were not entirely without benefit. Feudal leaders from Europe came into contact with civilizations superior to their own. The serfs gained some power over their lives. A few good laws were passed and the superstition coming out of the Catholic Church was diminished. In short, the stage was set for the Reformation.

Mackay next addresses the issue of two and a half centuries of European superstition, where the mass of people came to believe that certain individuals had the power to summon evil spirits at will. This madness led to a natural belief that if others could summon evil spirits, every calamity that occurred to a person was because of witchcraft.

If your cattle died or a storm blew down your barn or one of your children caught the plague, it had to be witchcraft. Many thousands of innocent people were killed, all in the belief they were witches. In some German cities, an average of two executions a day of convicted witches took place for years.

Naturally the very best way to determine if someone was under the control of the devil was to torture them. And in virtually every case, the accused did in fact prove to be an agent of the devil, and provided full details of the evil they had committed. It seemed not to matter to those judging that under torture people will confess to whatever you want to hear, just to make the torment stop.

Each country seemed to have its own favorite form of witch transport. In England and France the witches tended to prefer broomsticks. In Spain and Italy the devil turned into a goat and moved them around riding on his back. The devil and his henchmen, and henchwomen as it were, celebrated their Sabbath on Friday and Saturday. Witches couldn't go through doors or windows to get to the Sabbath, they made it in through keyholes and out through the chimney.

Each of the wizards and witches needed to prove obedience to the devil by literally kissing his ass, the devil having taken the form of a large he-goat. Each participant was carefully examined for the secret mark that would prove they belonged to the devil. Newcomers were made to deny "his salvation, kissed the devil, spat upon the Bible, and sworn obedience to him in all things."

It's amazing what a little torture will do to spur the creativity of those being tortured.

By 1307, the Templars, once honored as protectors of the faith, had created enough enemies through their wealth, power, pride and a remarkable degree of insolence that "the terrible cry of witchcraft was let loose upon them." Philip IV, King of France, ordered the arrest of all the Templars under his domain. No doubt his hatred of the Templars had nothing at all to do with the fact he was deeply in debt to the order and could not pay.

On Friday the thirteenth of October 1307, all the Templars who could be found were seized. Their arrest and later demise was the source of the superstition that Friday the thirteenth is an unlucky day. Certainly it seemed that way at least to them.

The Pope took up the cause in turn. All over Europe the Templars found themselves chucked into prison, with all their goods and possessions seized and turned over to the authorities.

Under torture, naturally the Templars confessed. Once removed from the rack, they often would deny the confessions, and just as naturally, when they refuted their confessions that too was promptly used against them.

You get arrested, you get tortured. You get tortured, you confess. You confess, you get executed. The only choice was to die after a lot of pain or to die without much pain. The wiser Templars promptly confessed once torture began.

In the last act of the farce, the Grand Master of the order, Jacques de Molay, was barbecued along with his last companions in March of 1314 in front of the Church of Notre Dame de Paris, on a small island in the River Seine. The wealth and papers of the Templars were never found.

Joan of Arc went to be burned at the stake based on her reports of having visions from the Archangel

Michael, St. Margret and St. Catherine telling her to support King Charles VII in his battle against the English. The yet uncrowned King sent her to the siege of Orléans as part of a relief mission in May of 1429. Within days the siege was lifted, in part due to her efforts, and the thankful soldiers gave her full credit for their victory.

Several more swift victories made it possible for the young ink to be crowned formally as king. Joan of Arc actually fought and was wounded in several of the actions.

A year later French forces allied with the English captured her. The French turned her over to the English and the bishop of Beauvais, Pierre Cauchon, accused her of witchcraft and heresy. Both heresy and witchcraft were the equivalent of conspiracy today. All you had to do was accuse someone and there was a presumption of guilt.

After a short but effective bout of torture Joan of Arc was found guilty and burned at the stake a week after her capture. She was all of nineteen years old.

As you continue to read deeper and deeper into *EPD* eventually you begin to realize that, gee, people are really stupid. They did one insane thing after another and everyone went along with the crowd. Yup, that's it, folks. That's what the whole book is about. If you read it, you are going to come eventually to the conclusion that people really are dumber than bricks.

And that's a big part of why you need to take most of the responsibility for your own investment decisions on yourself. People are dumb in general and nobody knows anything.

While we were taught that history books were filled with endless stories of the wisdom and bold leadership of kings, prime ministers and presidents, it's just not so. History books should be filled with what really goes on at those levels, and it's one dumb move after another.

Chapter 2
Contrarian Investing

MAN IS A HERD ANIMAL just as much as any of the birds or the beasts. If you have ever seen a flock of birds or a school of fish turn on a dime you must wonder just what it is that tells them all to do the same thing at the same time. As much as man would like to pretend that we are a superior species designed to lord over the rest of the creatures of the world, we share characteristics with all the other animals.

Over millions of years animals have learned to survive by joining together in herds to protect themselves from predators. Just what was it that sent the signal so the group knew what to do at a moment's notice? Herd behavior confuses predators as it becomes almost impossible for a predator to distinguish an individual target as it moves in and out of the mass of fish or birds or zebras.

While belonging to a herd may protect gazelles from lions in Africa and get dates for young people in college, it is the kiss of death for investors because of a simple mathematical equation.

Think of investing as a zero sum game. Yes, there are times when it is not so, but for purposes of illustration imagine half of all investors thinking gold is going to go up and the other half thinking it's going to go down. With one winner and one loser, 51 per cent have to lose because it's not really zero sum, as you have to allow for the spread between bid and ask and you have to factor in commissions. So if you want to invest with the herd, you will always lose money because the herd is the 51 per cent.

That was the fatal flaw with Long Term Capital Management back in 1998. LTCM thought they had invented the perpetual motion money machine that would print out crisp $100 bills every single day. For a long time it seemed they had. But the financial bets LTCM made grew so large, they became the market and the predators ate their lunch in a matter of speaking. They became the herd and the herd always gets eaten.

Understanding contrarian investing is simple and there are some excellent books about how to think and bet as a contrarian. Imagine there are one hundred people in a room, all thinking about the price of gold. If half of them think it will go up and half think it will go down, either or both will happen over time. There can be no contrarian opinion because one side balances the other. There is nothing to be contrarian against.

But what if war starts, the banks close, paper money loses all value and all of a sudden every single person in that room believes the price of gold will go up? What happens on the next trade?

The answer is that the price has to go down. When you run out of buyers, all you have left is sellers. The same is true at bottoms. When you run out of sellers, all those left become buyers.

And even someone who thinks gold is going to go up still has bills to pay, or a mortgage coming due, or sonny needs money for college or his secretary needs an abortion in a rush.

There is only one reason to buy any financial instrument. That is that you think it will go up. But there are hundreds of reasons to sell. So it happens that some will sell while convinced that prices will continue to go up.

You do not want to be part of the herd. The herd is always wrong (see Chapter 1) and 51 per cent of participants have to lose because of friction. That is just as true at tops as at bottoms.

At every top, there are one hundred fundamental reasons to buy. And at every bottom there are one hundred reasons to sell. That's what makes them tops and bottoms.

Markets discount the future. No one can know the future, but markets are made up of the collective wisdom of tens of millions of financial decisions made all over the world at any given moment by billions of people.

Contrary to the belief of those who believe markets can be controlled, the price of any market is correct at that moment in time, for every market. People who believe manipulation is significant also by definition believe that supply and demand doesn't work. Well, it does work. And markets constantly discount the future.

Price is always correct, opinions are often wrong.

Contrarian investing is one of the very few ways I know to make money. It's certainly the easiest, even if the least popular. You just have to figure out how to measure it.

In late April of 2011 I was monitoring the bullish consensus on silver. It went to a record high of 96 per cent bulls. To give you an idea of how important a top that was, the bullish consensus on silver on Monday January 22, 1980, when it hit an all-time high of $50.25 an ounce on the open, measured 94 per cent.

Eric Sprott had been doing a wonderful job of touting his Sprott Physical Silver Trust prior to April of 2011. When I wrote my piece, investors were paying a 25 per cent premium over the spot price of silver for his silver ETF. That's nuts.

If you went into a coin store and the owner offered you silver at a price 25 per cent over spot, you would know he was a crook. But people were voluntarily paying Eric Sprott that premium. That's a tribute both to his ability to market himself and to the stupidity of his investors.

It was a top, I said so, and then hundreds of people sent me some of the nastiest emails I have ever gotten. To each I suggested they wait awhile to see just who was right and then write me back. None did. Two weeks after that top, silver was down 35 per cent.

There were about five guys who got it dead right on silver in April of 2011 and I can guarantee all of them were using contrarian investing.

There were dozens of other signals available if you were capable of thinking for yourself (not many really are) and didn't listen to the noise coming from the herd.

Guys who had been selling refrigerators at Wal-Mart six months before started touting silver as if they had been born with a fist full of it. A dozen or more websites popped out of nowhere to begin taking orders for silver rounds. You could go to a party and people were talking about how high the price of silver was going to go.

Hint: Silver hit $4.01 an ounce in late November of 2001. It ran to just under $50 in late April of 2011. The smart money was booking profits. If you can buy something and make an 1,100 per cent profit, forget how much it's going up and focus on how much it's already gone up.

Silver was moving from strong hands into weak hands. That's what you want to do. At market tops the weak hands are buying, and at bottoms the weak hands are selling. You need know nothing about silver or gold or any other commodity. All you have to do is learn to measure investor psychology and behavior.

Contrarian investing is at its easiest and most profitable at market turns, in any market. You are looking for whatever would give you the very best signal of investor psychology. In March of 2000, as the NAZ was going up 19 days in a row (now that's a contrarian's dream signal), I saw two articles on the net. One was about a group of nuns who were holding stock picking contests. The other was about inmates in a jail in Baltimore holding stock picking contests.

There are things you can know without being told if you will just learn to think for yourself. You don't need this book, or me; all you need do is think.

When nuns and prison inmates are holding stock picking contests, you have totally run out of buyers. Whatever they are thinking of buying is at an absolute top; there is no dumber money anywhere in the known universe. That is a perfect signal and it proved accurate in March of 2000.

Another valuable measure of investor psychology would be the volume of trading. This is especially valuable in the trading of the "penny dreadful"; stocks of tiny companies with market caps under $50 million. It wouldn't be as valuable elsewhere due to the increased liquidity elsewhere.

The penny dreadfuls trade on psychology. When they are booming and going up every day, trading in an individual stock will be in the hundreds of thousands or even millions of shares a day. But when they are hated, days will go by without a single trade, or there will be a pitiful handful of thousands traded over a whole day.

That's a contrarian delight, for it gives an

intelligent investor a valuable signal. At bottoms you can wait for weeks for your order to be filled, while at tops you can get an execution in an instant. So when markets have collapsed for weeks, months and years, put in a "stink bid" below the market and wait for the price to come to you. Someone has to be the person to get the lowest price. Why shouldn't it be you?

Buy on low volume and sell on high volume. I know every other writer is doing their best to convince you of the fundamentals of the market and the quality of management and why such-and-such country is the next great thing, but those are all opinions and opinions are often wrong.

I've been on hundreds of mining tours and in every case I'm trying to get a feel for management. I've been lied to by experts. I think I've probably been lied to on every tour I have ever been on. And why not? They have had a lifetime of preparation. I've seen some great companies and great concepts destroyed. A sufficiently determined management can destroy the best projects.

So if I can't measure management and I know these guys, how are you going to figure it out? Go with what is simple and what works. When the trading volume on juniors is quiet, it's a far better time to buy than to sell. When trading volume is high, it's probably a better time to sell than to buy.

Another exceptionally valuable contrarian signal with the penny dreadfuls is simply the price. Many years ago I read of a stock market wizard who proclaimed that the road to riches was to buy low and sell high. My immediate reaction was, "Just how do you tell when it's low and when it's high?"

Actually that's very simple. All you have to do is look at a stock reporting service such as Stockwatch or Stockhouse. They report full details on all commonly traded shares. Included in the information is the yearly high and yearly low price.

If you look at the yearly prices of say 10 or 20 junior mining stocks, you will realize that the yearly range from the low to the high varies from 100 per cent to 1,000 per cent in normal years. The key to buying low and selling higher is that you have to trade. That is, you have to sell when you have a profit, not hold forever.

If I have made a mistake, and I have, over the past 15 years, it would be in not pressing harder for the owners of junior mining companies to take a profit when they can. Many investors buy at the right time, and buy the right company. They watch it go up 500 per cent and do nothing, content in the view that it's going to keep going up forever.

Let me show you one example, that of NovaGold. I started following NovaGold in the summer of 2001. In US dollars the price had been as low at $.09 in the spring and early summer. It was $.13 in Canadian pesos. It began to climb as people realized the gold bull market was on. The stock went up ten-fold, then twenty-fold, eventually going to $20.44 in 2007. Then with the great financial crash NovaGold began to drop, plummeting to $.46 in late 2008. New management injected money into the company and the shares got up to $16.60 by late 2010. The rollercoaster ride continued with NovaGold touching $1.99 in 2013 before getting to over $7 recently.

If you invest to make money rather than to fulfill your fantasies, there are dozens or hundreds of opportunities similar to that of NovaGold in the junior market. But you have to be a trader. You have to have the courage to buy low when no one else wants to buy and you have to be willing to take a profit. Few people do, but you can profit by their foolishness. If the slow moving stocks had a range of 100 per cent in a year, would you be satisfied with a 25 per cent return? If you would, try it. But you have to trade rather than sit on shares waiting for them to hatch.

Chapter 3
Deviation and Regression to the Mean

RELATIONSHIPS EXIST between both similar and dissimilar commodities. The ratio of the number of ounces of silver it takes to buy one ounce of gold varied from about 17:1 in January of 1980 to over 100:1 in early 1991. We view both metals as precious and having some aspects of money. But the ratio changes a lot and that creates an opportunity to profit without needing the ability to predict direction of price movement. You don't need to speculate on the commodities going up or down, only that they regress to a mean.

And it's not necessary for commodities to be similar. For some reason sugar and silver seem to move together much of the time. There is no necessity for a logical relationship in order for there to be an actual relationship.

To understand deviation from the mean, we first need some basic understanding of what makes prices change. That's easy. The answer is inflation. But inflation distorts price information and while eventually everything goes up because of inflation, things go up at different rates because the market doesn't know at any given time what the correct price is for anything and is constantly testing.

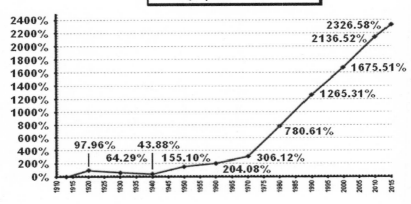

For each pair of commodities that we might seek to profit from there will be a different chart, but basically it's all about deviation from the mean of inflation and regression to the mean.

Going back over the past 100 years, if we chose to use silver vs. gold as our means of investing for a profit, the ratio has varied from 17:1 to 100:1 but had a mean of 53:1. Do remember that the price of gold was fixed at $20.67 an ounce until Roosevelt took the public off the gold standard in 1933 and revalued gold at $35 in January of 1934. While the price of silver varied between 1934 and 1971, gold remained relatively constant until Nixon took us totally off the gold standard in August of 1971. Since that time both metals have traded freely and have offered numerous opportunities to profit.

Spot Gold vs Spot Silver

There are a number of different ways an investor could have capitalized during the period shown in the chart. The first clear signal was when the silver to gold ratio went above 85, in 1995. Since there are more options now, I'll cover what the options were then.

Since you get many ounces of silver for each ounce of gold, one alternative for the punter is to sell gold and buy silver at the same time and in about the same dollar value. Twenty years ago pretty much the only choice was the use of commodity contracts. A ratio spread of buying silver/selling gold would have carried far less margin requirement than a naked position in either commodity. I'm going to use big numbers as an example but only because there were fewer options then.

A standard silver contract is 5,000 ounces and a standard gold contract is 100 ounces. On March 2, 1995 gold was $375 an ounce and silver was $4.40. The ratio of silver to gold was thus 85:1. There were also 1,000-ounce silver contracts available, so the thing to do would have been to short 100 ounces of gold and go long either 7,000 or 8,000 ounces of silver. Because of the reduced opportunities to trade various alternatives, you couldn't match the dollar amounts perfectly.

What is most important to understand about trading on deviation from the mean is that you do not need to make a directional bet. While it was true that silver was cheaper relative to gold, it didn't and doesn't necessarily mean that silver was going to go higher. Regression to the mean only means that it should go higher relative to gold. You don't really care if the metals go up or down, you only care that the relative value changes.

Another simple alternative would have been to just sell gold since it had deviated the most from the mean, and take the money from that to buy silver. That presumes the investor had a stash of gold.

The investor would have needed to stay in the investment for just about three years, for on February 6, 1998 gold went to $299 as silver hit $7.80 for a ratio of 38:1. So the investment above would have showed a profit of $76 an ounce for $7,600 on the gold short and $23,800 for the silver long. Obviously no one picks perfect tops and bottoms but what I'm trying to show is that by investing when ratios deviate from the mean, there can be a lot of profit.

If all the investor had done was to sell three ounces of gold in 1995 for a total of $1,125 and put that money into silver at $4.40, and then reversed the trade in 1998, he would have ended up with six ounces of gold in 1998. If you own gold, silver and platinum, you can continue to increase your total number of ounces at a relatively low risk. It's all based on historical data, deviation from the mean and regression to the mean.

The trade offered a second entry point in December of 1996. As long as the investor understands that all he is betting on is regression to the mean, this second entry point was nearly as good as the first. Understand that when the spread passes

80 it doesn't last long and there is no fundamental or technical reason for it to stay above 80. It's going to regress to the mean and beyond.

There was another buy silver/sell gold signal in mid-2003 that lasted until early 2006. And another buy gold/sell silver signal in 2007 that reversed direction in late 2008.

In 2011 silver shot higher, to almost $50 an ounce. Entry into the buy gold/sell silver at 45 would have been unprofitable for a few months, but sure enough silver went back to a ratio of 84:1 to gold in March of 2016, offering yet another trade.

These trades take years but returns of above 30-35 per cent are consistent and will remain so over the future. No matter what is happening in the economy, there is a relationship between the prices of gold and silver. While they may deviate from the mean, eventually they return to the mean.

We like to believe we can make profitable investments at no cost on our part but it's simply not so. When you are using deviation from the mean and regression to the mean as a source of signal, you need the basic data to make intelligent decisions. I've been on the web for over twenty years in one form or another. The very best source of information that I am aware of for charts showing deviation and regression would be that of sharelynx.com, run by the incredible Nick Laird from Australia.

Nick gives new readers a three-week trial for free.

If it gives you what you need, you have a choice of one year for $200 or two years for $360. A single trade would more than pay for your subscription.

Understanding deviation from the mean can be very valuable in other ways than just a single trade. For example I wrote a piece in early March of 2016 in which I pointed out that relative to commodities in general, the gold price was the highest it had been in history. Relative to 5,000 years of record keeping, commodities were cheaper in real terms than they had ever been. Platinum was selling at a $320 discount to gold, also a record low for platinum. Silver was selling at a ratio of 84 ounces for each ounce of gold. That was near the highest it had ever been. Oil had hit the highest ratio to gold it had ever been, at 48 barrels of oil to one ounce of gold. Even during the darkest days of the Great Depression oil was only 40 barrels per ounce. Clearly a few weeks ago we had a significant deviation from the mean.

Those are all signals. In the ten days since I wrote the piece and called gold expensive (in relative terms), platinum gained $45 on the spread, silver improved to an 80:1 ratio, and commodities shot up by 12 per cent. Oil advanced by an incredible 50 per cent in three weeks since its low at $26 a barrel. My point is not that I am so smart; I'm not any smarter than you. But all this information provides signals that will help you make more intelligent decisions about what to do with your money.

If an advisor isn't going to share your pain, why should you give him any of the gain? It's your money. The information is easy to find, and while the Internet is not the font of all wisdom, there is an incredible amount of valuable information if you will only learn to think and use the tools available to you.

It's vital that average investors realize that most of the information available to them on the web is noise. Everything you get from the mainstream media is noise designed to confuse rather than enlighten. And I mean everything. The mainstream media is so far past its sell-by date they should all resign and get real jobs. There is good information on the web but you have to sift out all the garbage. Investing based on the information you get from understanding relationships between commodities is fairly consistent.

If you trade the silver/gold spread, buying gold and selling silver has worked four times in the last twenty years if you use a ratio of 45:1. Buying silver and selling gold has worked five times in the last 20 years if you use a ratio of 80:1 to sell the gold and buy the silver. These are boring trades that you enter and just go to sleep. A trading signal that works every time and comes along every two years or so is not a bad deal. Consistent returns of over 33 per cent add up over time.

Just as a matter of interest, silver has been above 80:1 lately as I write in March of 2016 and there's a wonderful opportunity to profit. You can buy silver and not need the excuse of manipulation or a massive conspiracy to justify your investment.

The cornucopia of ETFs may well be the death of the world's financial system but it's far easier to trade today than ever before. You can buy or sell the ETFs for silver or gold or oil or platinum or palladium. You can still trade commodities if your budget is higher, or you can simply trade in and out of a particular commodity if you have an account with an offshore metals storage facility. In many cases, the spread between bid and ask can be as little as a few percent. If you want to own metals for the long term, you can be trading with no more than a few ounces of gold. This is not just a rich man's trade.

And, if for no other reason, it gives you an idea of what is really going on. We have been hearing for many months that we are in for more and more deflation. But when you know as a matter of fact that commodities are the cheapest they have been in history, it doesn't take a brain surgeon to realize prices have to go up no matter what the talking heads say. If you actually read *EPD*, you know just how much credibility you should give to the talking heads.

This isn't just interesting information, it's a way to make it through a minefield filled with booby traps designed to pluck the tail feathers off the ordinary investor. For example, when gold rocketed higher to $1,923 an ounce in September of 2011, a chart from sharelynx.com showed that in comparison to all other metals, gold was higher in relative terms than it had been going all the way back to 1950. That was a clear and convincing signal to sell gold. It was expensive not only in relative terms but in actual terms.

Likewise when the Sprott Physical Silver ETF was trading at a 25 per cent premium to silver in April of 2011. You could look at the premium that the Sprott Physical Gold ETF had to gold and it wasn't much. And you could look at the premium that the Sprott Physical Platinum and Palladium ETF had to those metals and realize that silver was sort of all by itself. People were willing to pay a 25 per cent premium over spot in the silver ETF but not the others. It was a tribute to the ability of Eric Sprott to convince people to pay a lot more for silver than it was really worth. But it was a top. Look for that sort of information. You don't need an expert; you can figure it out yourself.

One of the most valuable charts you will ever see will be a relative performance chart of various commodities. You will often see these as charts of other investments such as rare paintings, diamonds, gold, real estate or any other type of investment. The signal these charts show us is how much each investment has gained or lost over the length of time measured in the chart.

The chart shown is for March 17, 2016 and came from Barcharts.com. It measures the gains and losses in all commodities since the beginning of 2016. It's important to note here that to get an accurate signal, you need to measure relative performance over a reasonable period of time.

The chart on the next page shows only the period from January of 2016 to mid-March. Since the commodity that has gone down the most is natural gas, it's not a perfectly reasonable period to select. Natural gas almost always goes down at the end of winter.

What I am trying to show is the type of chart measuring different commodities. They are always moving and something is always overpriced and something else is always underpriced. The chart shows the relative value over a timeframe, not absolute price. You can't look at the chart and say gold should go down. But it's a hint that gold is overpriced over a three-month timeframe compared to natural gas. You always want to know where you are in relative terms. You don't have to trade anything but you can trade everything. Selling what is expensive and buying what is cheap is a low-risk, high-potential area of profit and you don't need a guru to tell you what to do.

Barcharts.com has an excellent service and I highly recommend them or any other similar charting service. This isn't magic, it's just using the tools that we all have available to us.

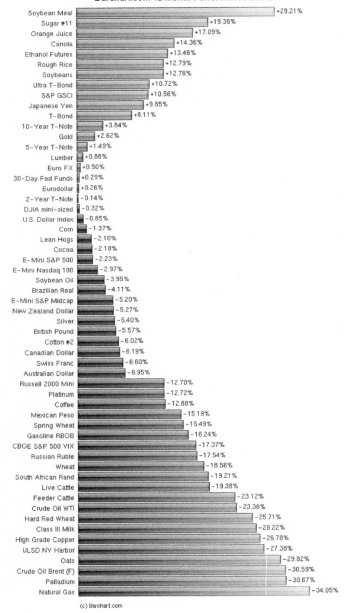

Barchart.com 12-Month Performance Leaders

Commodity	Performance
Soybean Meal	+29.21%
Sugar #11	+19.36%
Orange Juice	+17.09%
Canola	+14.36%
Ethanol Futures	+13.46%
Rough Rice	+12.79%
Soybeans	+12.76%
Ultra T-Bond	+10.72%
S&P GSCI	+10.56%
Japanese Yen	+9.85%
T-Bond	+8.11%
10-Year T-Note	+3.84%
Gold	+2.62%
5-Year T-Note	+1.49%
Lumber	+0.88%
Euro FX	+0.50%
30-Day Fed Funds	+0.29%
Eurodollar	+0.26%
2-Year T-Note	-0.14%
DJIA mini-sized	-0.32%
U.S. Dollar Index	-0.85%
Corn	-1.37%
Lean Hogs	-2.10%
Cocoa	-2.18%
E-Mini S&P 500	-2.23%
E-Mini Nasdaq 100	-2.97%
Soybean Oil	-3.95%
Brazilian Real	-4.11%
E-Mini S&P Midcap	-5.20%
New Zealand Dollar	-5.27%
Silver	-5.40%
British Pound	-5.57%
Cotton #2	-6.02%
Canadian Dollar	-6.19%
Swiss Franc	-6.60%
Australian Dollar	-6.95%
Russell 2000 Mini	-12.70%
Platinum	-12.72%
Coffee	-12.86%
Mexican Peso	-15.19%
Spring Wheat	-15.49%
Gasoline RBOB	-16.24%
CBOE S&P 500 VIX	-17.37%
Russian Ruble	-17.54%
Wheat	-18.56%
South African Rand	-19.21%
Live Cattle	-19.38%
Feeder Cattle	-23.12%
Crude Oil WTI	-23.36%
Hard Red Wheat	-25.71%
Class III Milk	-26.22%
High Grade Copper	-26.78%
ULSD NY Harbor	-27.38%
Oats	-29.82%
Crude Oil Brent (F)	-30.59%
Palladium	-30.67%
Natural Gas	-34.05%

(c) Barchart.com

50

Another really valuable financial site is that of Finviz.com. Don't bother asking me how to pronounce it; I'm certain it sorta rolls off your tongue. Finviz.com calls itself a financial visualization site. They have tons of information about stocks, bonds, commodities, financial futures, and just about anything else. Their performance charts under the heading of Futures are especially valuable. Now these charts are not nearly as clear or as valuable a signal as that of a chart of silver vs. gold. With the silver/gold ratio it's very easy to see a clear and convincing signal when the ratio gets above 80 or below 45. But you may well determine that you want to use some other arbitrary number as your signal.

With the Finviz.com data you are seeing relative price performance for a variety of timeframes, and that is important. For example, the relative performance for one day is pretty meaningless. It would almost fall into the random number category. No one can get a clear and convincing signal from one day's trading in anything.

The data and the value of the signal increase over time. For example, as we see on the following pages, natural gas was the worst performer in the year-to-date chart, the six-month performance chart, and the one-year relative performance chart. To my not very great surprise, natural gas was the best performer over a one-week period.

It is natural that what performs the best over a

long period will naturally perform the worst over a subsequent and corresponding period of time. No broker or financial writer will tell you this but they all know it.

These do not generate trading signals but they can give you a feel for what should happen over a period of time. If diamonds go up the most over a five-year period, it would be common for them to go down the most over the following five-year period.

Part of my point is that all financial markets go up and down. When someone is trying to convince you that a market is one-way and can only go up or can only go down, you will know they don't know what they are talking about.

It is the nature of markets, all markets, to wander up and down. Finding the correct price for anything at a given point in time is akin to trying to throw darts at a target in a totally dark room. Markets go up, markets go down, and in time they determine what the correct price is for everything.

The charts on the following eight pages all came from Finviz.com.

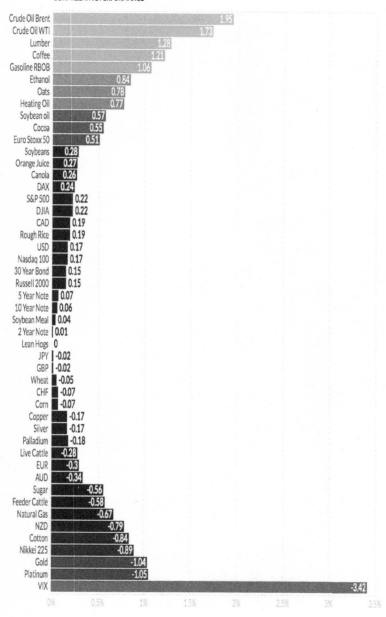

1 DAY RELATIVE PERFORMANCE

Crude Oil Brent	1.95
Crude Oil WTI	1.73
Lumber	1.28
Coffee	1.21
Gasoline RBOB	1.06
Ethanol	0.84
Oats	0.78
Heating Oil	0.77
Soybean oil	0.57
Cocoa	0.55
Euro Stoxx 50	0.51
Soybeans	0.28
Orange Juice	0.27
Canola	0.26
DAX	0.24
S&P 500	0.22
DJIA	0.22
CAD	0.19
Rough Rice	0.19
USD	0.17
Nasdaq 100	0.17
30 Year Bond	0.15
Russell 2000	0.15
5 Year Note	0.07
10 Year Note	0.06
Soybean Meal	0.04
2 Year Note	0.01
Lean Hogs	0
JPY	-0.02
GBP	-0.02
Wheat	-0.05
CHF	-0.07
Corn	-0.07
Copper	-0.17
Silver	-0.17
Palladium	-0.18
Live Cattle	-0.28
EUR	-0.3
AUD	-0.34
Sugar	-0.56
Feeder Cattle	-0.58
Natural Gas	-0.67
NZD	-0.79
Cotton	-0.84
Nikkei 225	-0.89
Gold	-1.04
Platinum	-1.05
VIX	-3.42

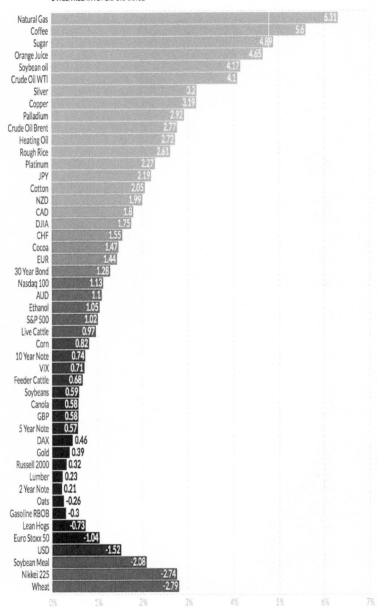

1 WEEK RELATIVE PERFORMANCE

Natural Gas	6.31
Coffee	5.6
Sugar	4.89
Orange Juice	4.65
Soybean oil	4.17
Crude Oil WTI	4.1
Silver	3.2
Copper	3.19
Palladium	2.92
Crude Oil Brent	2.77
Heating Oil	2.72
Rough Rice	2.61
Platinum	2.27
JPY	2.19
Cotton	2.05
NZD	1.99
CAD	1.8
DJIA	1.75
CHF	1.55
Cocoa	1.47
EUR	1.44
30 Year Bond	1.28
Nasdaq 100	1.13
AUD	1.1
Ethanol	1.05
S&P 500	1.02
Live Cattle	0.97
Corn	0.82
10 Year Note	0.74
VIX	0.71
Feeder Cattle	0.68
Soybeans	0.59
Canola	0.58
GBP	0.58
5 Year Note	0.57
DAX	0.46
Gold	0.39
Russell 2000	0.32
Lumber	0.23
2 Year Note	0.21
Oats	-0.26
Gasoline RBOB	-0.3
Lean Hogs	-0.73
Euro Stoxx 50	-1.04
USD	-1.52
Soybean Meal	-2.08
Nikkei 225	-2.74
Wheat	-2.79

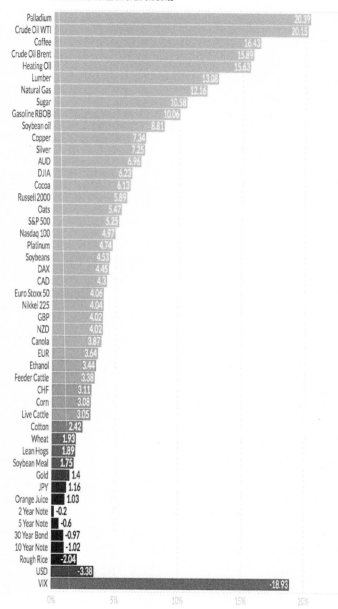

MONTH TO DATE RELATIVE PERFORMANCE

Palladium	20.39
Crude Oil WTI	20.15
Coffee	16.43
Crude Oil Brent	15.89
Heating Oil	15.63
Lumber	13.08
Natural Gas	12.16
Sugar	10.58
Gasoline RBOB	10.06
Soybean oil	8.81
Copper	7.34
Silver	7.25
AUD	6.96
DJIA	6.23
Cocoa	6.13
Russell 2000	5.89
Oats	5.47
S&P 500	5.25
Nasdaq 100	4.97
Platinum	4.74
Soybeans	4.53
DAX	4.45
CAD	4.3
Euro Stoxx 50	4.06
Nikkei 225	4.04
GBP	4.02
NZD	4.02
Canola	3.87
EUR	3.64
Ethanol	3.44
Feeder Cattle	3.38
CHF	3.11
Corn	3.08
Live Cattle	3.05
Cotton	2.42
Wheat	1.93
Lean Hogs	1.89
Soybean Meal	1.75
Gold	1.4
JPY	1.16
Orange Juice	1.03
2 Year Note	-0.2
5 Year Note	-0.6
30 Year Bond	-0.97
10 Year Note	-1.02
Rough Rice	-2.04
USD	-3.38
VIX	-18.93

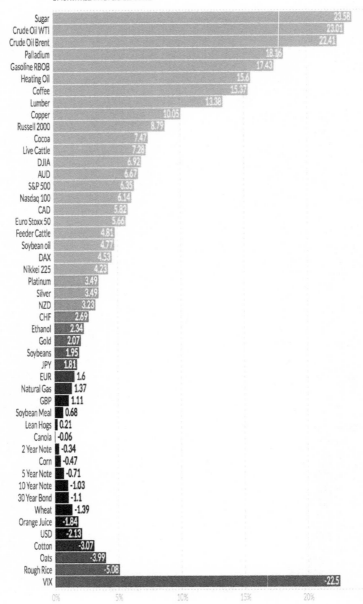

1 MONTH RELATIVE PERFORMANCE

Sugar	23.58
Crude Oil WTI	23.01
Crude Oil Brent	22.41
Palladium	18.36
Gasoline RBOB	17.43
Heating Oil	15.6
Coffee	15.37
Lumber	13.38
Copper	10.05
Russell 2000	8.79
Cocoa	7.47
Live Cattle	7.28
DJIA	6.92
AUD	6.67
S&P 500	6.35
Nasdaq 100	6.14
CAD	5.82
Euro Stoxx 50	5.66
Feeder Cattle	4.81
Soybean oil	4.77
DAX	4.53
Nikkei 225	4.23
Platinum	3.49
Silver	3.49
NZD	3.23
CHF	2.69
Ethanol	2.34
Gold	2.07
Soybeans	1.95
JPY	1.81
EUR	1.6
Natural Gas	1.37
GBP	1.11
Soybean Meal	0.68
Lean Hogs	0.21
Canola	-0.06
2 Year Note	-0.34
Corn	-0.47
5 Year Note	-0.71
10 Year Note	-1.03
30 Year Bond	-1.1
Wheat	-1.39
Orange Juice	-1.84
USD	-2.13
Cotton	-3.07
Oats	-3.99
Rough Rice	-5.08
VIX	-22.5

0%   5%   10%   15%   20%   25%

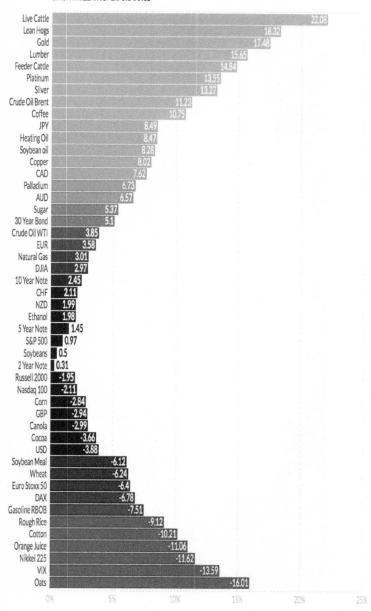

3 MONTH RELATIVE PERFORMANCE

Live Cattle	22.08
Lean Hogs	18.32
Gold	17.48
Lumber	15.65
Feeder Cattle	14.84
Platinum	13.55
Silver	13.27
Crude Oil Brent	11.23
Coffee	10.75
JPY	8.49
Heating Oil	8.47
Soybean oil	8.28
Copper	8.02
CAD	7.62
Palladium	6.73
AUD	6.57
Sugar	5.37
30 Year Bond	5.1
Crude Oil WTI	3.85
EUR	3.58
Natural Gas	3.01
DJIA	2.97
10 Year Note	2.45
CHF	2.11
NZD	1.99
Ethanol	1.98
5 Year Note	1.45
S&P 500	0.97
Soybeans	0.5
2 Year Note	0.31
Russell 2000	-1.95
Nasdaq 100	-2.11
Corn	-2.84
GBP	-2.94
Canola	-2.99
Cocoa	-3.66
USD	-3.88
Soybean Meal	-6.12
Wheat	-6.24
Euro Stoxx 50	-6.4
DAX	-6.78
Gasoline RBOB	-7.51
Rough Rice	-9.12
Cotton	-10.21
Orange Juice	-11.06
Nikkei 225	-11.62
VIX	-13.59
Oats	-16.01

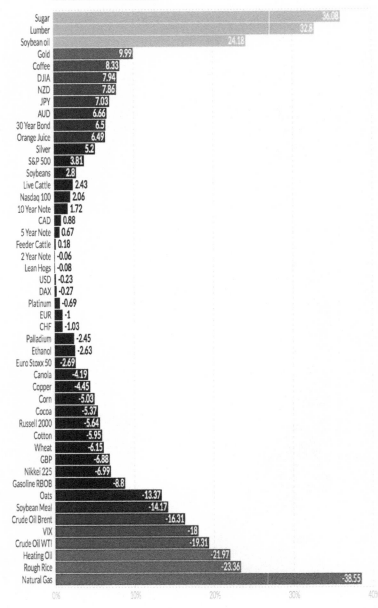

HALF YEAR RELATIVE PERFORMANCE

Sugar	36.08
Lumber	32.8
Soybean oil	24.18
Gold	9.99
Coffee	8.33
DJIA	7.94
NZD	7.86
JPY	7.03
AUD	6.66
30 Year Bond	6.5
Orange Juice	6.49
Silver	5.2
S&P 500	3.81
Soybeans	2.8
Live Cattle	2.43
Nasdaq 100	2.06
10 Year Note	1.72
CAD	0.88
5 Year Note	0.67
Feeder Cattle	0.18
2 Year Note	-0.06
Lean Hogs	-0.08
USD	-0.23
DAX	-0.27
Platinum	-0.69
EUR	-1
CHF	-1.03
Palladium	-2.45
Ethanol	-2.63
Euro Stoxx 50	-2.69
Canola	-4.19
Copper	-4.45
Corn	-5.03
Cocoa	-5.37
Russell 2000	-5.64
Cotton	-5.95
Wheat	-6.15
GBP	-6.88
Nikkei 225	-6.99
Gasoline RBOB	-8.8
Oats	-13.37
Soybean Meal	-14.17
Crude Oil Brent	-16.31
VIX	-18
Crude Oil WTI	-19.31
Heating Oil	-21.97
Rough Rice	-23.36
Natural Gas	-38.55

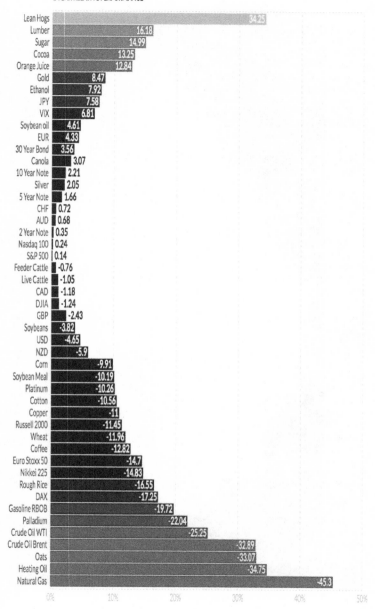

1 YEAR RELATIVE PERFORMANCE

Lean Hogs	34.25
Lumber	16.18
Sugar	14.99
Cocoa	13.25
Orange Juice	12.84
Gold	8.47
Ethanol	7.92
JPY	7.58
VIX	6.81
Soybean oil	4.61
EUR	4.33
30 Year Bond	3.56
Canola	3.07
10 Year Note	2.21
Silver	2.05
5 Year Note	1.66
CHF	0.72
AUD	0.68
2 Year Note	0.35
Nasdaq 100	0.24
S&P 500	0.14
Feeder Cattle	-0.76
Live Cattle	-1.05
CAD	-1.18
DJIA	-1.24
GBP	-2.43
Soybeans	-3.82
USD	-4.65
NZD	-5.9
Corn	-9.91
Soybean Meal	-10.19
Platinum	-10.26
Cotton	-10.56
Copper	-11
Russell 2000	-11.45
Wheat	-11.96
Coffee	-12.82
Euro Stoxx 50	-14.7
Nikkei 225	-14.83
Rough Rice	-16.55
DAX	-17.25
Gasoline RBOB	-19.72
Palladium	-22.04
Crude Oil WTI	-25.25
Crude Oil Brent	-32.89
Oats	-33.07
Heating Oil	-34.75
Natural Gas	-45.3

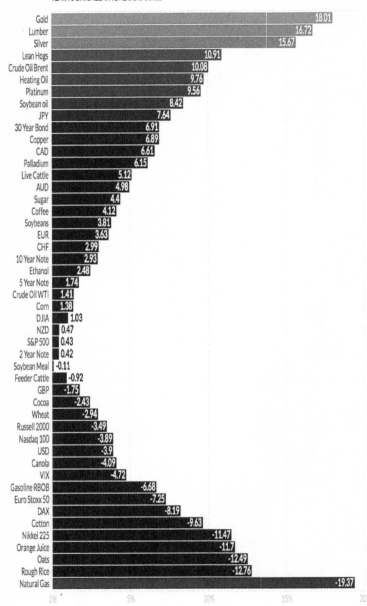

YEAR TO DATE RELATIVE PERFORMANCE

Gold	18.01
Lumber	16.72
Silver	15.67
Lean Hogs	10.91
Crude Oil Brent	10.08
Heating Oil	9.76
Platinum	9.56
Soybean oil	8.42
JPY	7.64
30 Year Bond	6.91
Copper	6.89
CAD	6.61
Palladium	6.15
Live Cattle	5.12
AUD	4.98
Sugar	4.4
Coffee	4.12
Soybeans	3.81
EUR	3.63
CHF	2.99
10 Year Note	2.93
Ethanol	2.48
5 Year Note	1.74
Crude Oil WTI	1.41
Corn	1.38
DJIA	1.03
NZD	0.47
S&P 500	0.43
2 Year Note	0.42
Soybean Meal	-0.11
Feeder Cattle	-0.92
GBP	-1.75
Cocoa	-2.43
Wheat	-2.94
Russell 2000	-3.49
Nasdaq 100	-3.89
USD	-3.9
Canola	-4.09
VIX	-4.72
Gasoline RBOB	-6.68
Euro Stoxx 50	-7.25
DAX	-8.19
Cotton	-9.63
Nikkei 225	-11.47
Orange Juice	-11.7
Oats	-12.49
Rough Rice	-12.76
Natural Gas	-19.37

Chapter 4
Delphi Polls

THERE IS A WAY for a group of people to come to a conclusion called a Delphi Poll. I became aware of it over fifty years ago when I was going through Marine Corps boot camp. I'm a little surprised that I've not heard other writers speak of it because it provides interesting information.

Imagine if you will being in combat and taking fire from a hilltop you can see but cannot hit with rifle or machine gun fire. You want to convince the enemy to stop shooting at you. One weapon available to small units in the military is the mortar. But to use the mortar effectively, you have to have some idea of what the distance is to a particular point.

One way to do it is to guess. But if you guess, you will be either short or long the distance. So if you presume people will either guess long or short, you could have half a dozen people guess the distance and then average those guesses. Some will probably be short and the others will be long but on average, you come up with a pretty close estimate.

It becomes even more effective if each individual makes his first guess independent of the group. But when you have come up with a number that represents the average, you allow people to change their estimates. The average of these second guesses will be even more accurate.

When you are measuring anything objective, and the distance from you to a distant hilltop is objective, which is to say it is fixed and can be measured, Delphi Polls are extremely accurate.

But what would happen if you got a thousand stock analysts together in a room at a convention and asked them to predict the stock that would go up the most in the next year?

That's a subjective view, not objective. Naturally each participant has his own biases. We always love our stocks the best. In this case, a Delphi Poll will not accurately determine the best stock to be buying; it will determine the worst stock to own over the next year because everyone votes his or her own book.

This has been done a number of times and they always give it up because it proves that with subjective polls, the participants always get it dead wrong.

So the next time you are tuned into mainstream media and the talking head announces, "Experts polled today all agree that Apple shares will be the leading gainer over the next year," you know you can call your broker and put in a short for Apple and can be confident of making money over the next year. The experts have spoken and they are always wrong.

Chapter 5
Bias and Agendas

THE MEDIA AND MANY WRITERS want to convince you that they are unbiased and have no agenda. That's utter rubbish. Everyone has some bias and most often they have an agenda. If you are not aware of that agenda you will give them a lot more credibility than you would if you understood what they are really trying to accomplish.

One of the biggest gurus in the silver space has been complaining for many years about position limits and how the COMEX is ignoring its own rules and how silver is the most manipulated commodity in history. If you knew that this particular guru had been thrown out of commodities permanently because of exceeding position limits on orange juice when he tried to corner the market, you might understand just how much credibility you should give him.

Does he want to get even with the CFTC? Of course.

Bill Murphy of GATA, received the second biggest fine in CFTC history and a permanent ban for doing to 94 of his clients what Hillary Clinton's broker did for her when she turned $1,000 into $100,000 literally overnight.

Back in those days, trades were unallocated. Hillary's broker entered two orders each morning.

One was to sell futures and the other was to buy exactly the same futures at the same time. Naturally when the positions were closed the trade was a wash. The loser offset the winner.

Since the objective of the entire exercise was to bribe Hillary for $100,000, the losing trades went into the house account and all of the winning trades went into Hillary's account.

Murphy did the same thing with 94 of his clients. But in this case, he kept the winning trades. The only flaw in the ointment was the fact that anyone smart enough to have a big commodity trading account is going to start looking very carefully into the specifics when 100 per cent of his trades are losers. He was stealing.

In the case of Murphy, he lost his license, got thrown out of the business permanently and was fined. Do you think maybe he wants to get even with the CFTC?

Fox News claims to be "Fair & Balanced" and goes on to claim, "We report. You decide." If you believe that, I have this wonderful, slightly used bridge in Brooklyn I'd make you a special deal on.

Studies show that 94 per cent of the viewers of Fox News identify themselves as Republicans. I wouldn't have any particular problem with Fox saying they have both a bias and an agenda, but claiming to be fair and balanced is an insult to the intelligence of anyone with an IQ over room temperature.

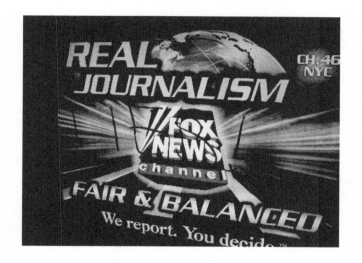

Everyone. Absolutely. Everyone. Has. A. Bias.

They may not even be aware of it, but they all have a bias. And most people have agendas. When you are listening to someone talk about an investment you need to be asking yourself, what is his bias and does he have an agenda? Most people do, and you need to take that into account. Their agenda is almost never to make money for you, and their bias is to do the best they can to line their own pockets.

Chapter 6
Reliance on Gurus

THERE ARE NO GURUS, there are only frauds claiming to be gurus. This is going to make me very unpopular because we all hate it when someone bursts our bubbles, but there are no gurus.

Lots of people want to claim to be gurus but the ability to market bullshit is not the same as the ability to make money for people. Some of the biggest names in finance are little more than charlatans claiming to be gurus, but eventually people figure out they have never made money for their listeners or readers and never will.

If you are really a guru, you ought to get it right now and again. It's nothing short of amazing that the most popular of the gurus have never gotten any prediction correct.

Why do we love gurus? What is it about gurus that makes us want to follow their every word and do everything they tell us to do?

Gurus are like politicians. They tell us the lies we want to hear. We all understand intuitively that no one would ever vote for an honest politician, in the unlikely event one could be found. Likewise with gurus, we want to follow the people who tell us exactly what we want to hear. It doesn't have to be correct, ever. If you feed people's fantasies, they will vote for you every time. When is the last time you heard of a guru being called to task for getting it dead wrong? It never happens to them, any more than it happens with politicians. As long as you tell people just want they want to hear, you can literally get away with murder.

How is it that blowing up a wedding party in Afghanistan with a drone strike is "defending America"?

Who cares?

Not Americans. So a few gooks get killed, but our military is protecting us in our beds from an attack from those nasty people.

Are you kidding? At one point a couple of years ago, the US military was fighting seven different wars in seven countries at the same time. Gee, the US must have a lot of enemies.

Do we hold politicians responsible for what they do? Not a chance. France and Hillary were responsible for dragging the US into involvement in Libya. Libya was the richest and best-run country in Africa. It literally was a model of democracy and a brilliant demonstration of how to use a country's wealth to improve the lives of its citizens.

The politicians got involved because of their own agenda. Now Libya is a cesspool run by warlords. Those responsible for the debacle are all staring at the ceiling and whistling "Dixie" and hoping no one notices what they have done.

Neither politicians nor gurus give a damn about you. I trust politicians about as far as I can throw them and gurus even less. When you see that someone has elected himself a guru, don't walk away, run. Their ability to market themselves doesn't correlate well with increases in your bank balance.

The fact that someone is telling you exactly what you want to hear is not a good thing, it's a bad thing. Hang on to your wallet carefully.

One of the very best reasons for following gurus is that you have someone to blame when your investment goes sour. I've seen a lot of that. Gurus are supposed to predict every twist and turn in the market, and so when they don't, it's not the investor's fault he lost money. It's the guru's fault.

Gurus don't care if you make money. They care if they make money. If you lose money it's because you made poor decisions. Make better decisions. One of the best you can make is to ignore all gurus.

Chapter 7
When to Sell

EVEN IF YOU IGNORE the rest of the book, memorize this chapter. You can have the touch of Midas in every investment you will ever make, but if you don't learn when to sell you will lose it all.

There is only one reason to buy any investment. That's because you think it will go up. However, there are ten thousand or more reasons to sell. You want a new car, you want to buy your partner some really wonderful flowers, you want to go on a special vacation, you died and the estate needs the money.

But there is something you have to understand about selling and I'm going to tell you a few stories so you get it.

I got back from Vietnam and left the Marine Corps in May of 1970. I promptly let my hair grow as fast as it could and I set out to travel around California on a Honda 350 motorcycle. The sister of my best friend in high school worked as a blackjack dealer in Tahoe so I rode up to spend a few days visiting her.

She was working the evening shift when I got there so I strolled over to the crap table to earn some money. I can teach anyone how to shoot craps and win in a few minutes if they are willing to listen so I don't consider myself to be actually gambling at the craps table; I'm just earning money.

In any case my friend got off work just as the dice came my way. I bet the same way I always do and made half a dozen passes before losing the dice. I picked up my chips and got ready to leave. My work was finished.

She said, "You can play longer if you want. I don't mind."

I said, "I always quit when I'm winning. I'm winning now so it's time to leave."

She replied wisely, "I see hundreds of gamblers come in here daily and some of them win a lot of money. Most of them just keep playing. You seem to have learned that if you don't take your money off the table when you are ahead, the only other alternative is to lose it all."

I already knew that. I had learned that in boot camp, shooting dice made up by another fool from pieces of chalk.

I got out of gold and silver a week early in January of 1980. On January 22 gold peaked at $875 and silver at $50.25 on the open. I got out around the fifteenth and left a lot of money on the table. However, I had been buying gold at $100 an ounce and silver at under $5, so what did I care about leaving some money behind?

In 1984 I needed a job so I went to work for a commodities company in Miami, Florida. That was an interesting experience. They repeated constantly, "We can make money, you can make money and the customer can make money. And two out of three isn't that bad."

You had to do a lot of cold calling and that was pretty brutal. The company had boxes of records from investors who had gotten caught up in the silver and gold boom of 1976 to 1980. I went through them looking for potential investors to call, in the hopes they might still be interested in investing in gold or silver.

What I found while going through the records was nothing short of remarkable. I saw hundreds of records of investors who had put in as little as $5,000 in 1978 and who were up $50,000 to $1 million in January of 1980.

So ask yourself a trick question. How many of those people who had made so much money actually took home a profit? The answer in every single case was the same. They not only didn't make money, they all lost everything they started with because they wouldn't sell.

If they had invested $50,000 and it went to a million, they lost it all. If they had invested $10,000 and it went to $250,000, they lost it all.

Because they ignored what my friend from the casino near Lake Tahoe had learned over years of watching people gamble.

If you aren't willing to take a profit, the only alternative is to take a loss.

I believe silver, gold, platinum, palladium and

rhodium are going to go into a bubble that will make the NAZ stock market bubble of 2000 look like a Monopoly game. And the people who will lose the most money will be the bulls. Because they will never take money off the table. They always want to keep betting. Eventually the house odds win out and they lose it all.

A fellow called me one day in 2004. He had been following one stock that I had written about a couple of times since 2001. He had bought a bunch of shares at $.11 and the stock was now $.75. He asked me what he should do.

First of all, I am not a registered rep, I don't make recommendations and I wasn't managing money for this guy. But he asked me a question and it was fair that I answer. So I did, by asking him a question.

"Sir, why did you buy the stock? What did you want it to do?" I asked.

"Well, I want to make money. I thought the stock looked good and I want it to go up," he responded.

"OK, here's what I would do," I continued. "I can't tell you what to do but here is what I would do. Sell the stock. If you got in it to make money and you are up 600 per cent in a year or so, it would be a good move to sell the shares and take the profit."

My advice was good. As it happened, the stock topped at $.76, problems popped up out of nowhere and the stock fell into the crapper.

A couple of years later I got a call from a farmer

in Kansas who had some questions. We chatted for a few minutes before I realized his voice was familiar. Sure enough, it was the guy who had called me for advice on what he should do with his stock.

He hadn't mentioned the prior call and I thought that was a little strange, so I said, "Aren't you the fellow who called me a couple of years back about that other stock?"

He replied, "Why, yes I am. And thank you for your wise advice."

I had to ask the question in the back of my mind. "But what did you do? When you called me the shares were seventy-five cents, and they topped at seventy-six before crashing. Did you get out?"

There was what you might call a long, pregnant silence before he answered. "Well." He paused. "Well, I finally sold those shares."

He took so long to answer that I knew I wasn't getting the whole story. So I asked another question. "And what was the average price you got for your shares?"

There was another long and pregnant pause that told me everything I needed to know.

"Well, I got rid of them at five cents a share."

"Damn," I said. "What were you thinking? You asked me for advice, I gave it and you ignored it. And by not being willing to sell at seventy-five you got sold out at the very low."

"I know," he answered. "They had gone up so

much, so fast, I thought they would just keep going up. Once they started down, I wanted to wait to sell until they were back at seventy-five."

If you don't take a profit when you can, you are going to take a loss when you have to. It's the only alternative to taking a profit.

My best friend in Miami is Colonel Sanders' grandson. His brother owned KFC of Florida for years before selling out to KFC of the United States around 1980. He made a lot of money and wasn't opposed to spending it. He and his third trophy wife had three major homes and half a dozen condos in Aspen.

On Mother's Day in 1982 Harland suggested I charter a plane and take them to Nassau for the weekend, all expenses paid. His lovely bride perked up and clapped. "Oh good, I've always wanted to win a jackpot in the slots. I want to go. How soon can we get on a plane?"

She was a beauty and I wanted to impress her. "Do you really want to win a jackpot?" I asked.

"Yes, oh yes. I've played the slots for years and never won a jackpot. I want to win one jackpot in my life. I want to make some money rather than giving it all to the house," she replied.

"OK, I can show you how to do that. You have to do exactly what I tell you to do, and when I tell you to do it, but I can help you win a jackpot. OK?"

I called a friend who had a plane I could borrow, we loaded our bags and off we went to Nassau. It was still cool in Miami but Nassau was brisk and breezy. We intended to make the most of our holiday.

After checking into our hotel rooms we agreed to take a rest and meet in the casino at seven to plan out the evening. At the appointed time we sat down for a drink and I told Scarlett just how to win a jackpot at the slots.

"Scarlett, they rig the machines nearest to the doors for a higher payout. Those machines pay out more money and there will be more jackpots on them because they are trying to lure people into the casino."

She was listening intently. "So what do I do?" she asked of me.

"Change twenty bucks into quarters and let's find a machine nearest to the doors," I instructed.

She came over near the doors holding a plastic cup with eighty quarters in it. We picked a machine and she sat down. The machine would take up to five quarters at a time so she quickly fed in five and got ready to pull the lever. Back in those days the slot machines actually had levers. Now people are so lazy that all they can be bothered to do is push a button.

She turned to me with a smile that would have melted an ice cube as she said, "Wish me luck." She pulled. And didn't win a thing. She loaded up the machine with another five quarters and gave it an honest yank. This time it came up four cherries and a $200 jackpot. She had invested $2.50 and made $200 in two minutes. That's a nice rate of return on investment. Sort of.

She literally jumped up and down with joy. This was her goal and she had won a big jackpot. In the scheme of things it didn't mean much, for the three of us used to go out to dinner a lot in Miami and $200 was a cheap dinner and drinks for the evening. But she wanted it and I had showed her how.

She literally had to go find a giant bucket to hold all the stupid quarters she had won. I watched the machine and her money while she was gone. When she came back she wanted to know if she should play the same machine or one of the others next to it.

"Scarlett, remember that I told you I would help you make money by winning a jackpot and you told me you would do exactly what I said?" I asked patiently.

"Of course I do," she answered with a smile.

"OK. Take all your quarters over to the cash window and turn them in for paper money. You wanted to win a jackpot, and you have. To keep the money, you now have to stop playing."

The smile fell off her face. "But I was winning. I want to play some more. I'll win another jackpot and stop then."

"Scarlett, shooting dice or playing the slots is as easy a way to make money as any I know of, but the key to winning is to walk away a winner. If you won't walk away when you are winning, the only alternative is that you will walk away when you are losing."

She looked at me with a pout. "But I'm having fun. I want to gamble. You go have a drink and I'll win a jackpot and be right over."

I wandered over to where her husband was sitting in the bar. He was on a liquid diet so we drank our dinner as we waited patiently. After a few hours Scarlett sauntered over swinging her now empty bucket of quarters. She had managed to blow through $220 in quarters. She won one jackpot and never did pull another winner. She had lots of little winners but the house odds were against her and eventually ate into her pot.

People invest in the junior mining stocks, otherwise well known as the penny dreadfuls, because they want a shot at making a 1,000 per cent return. If you can accurately call a bottom in a market like gold, as I did in May of 2001, you can find dozens of shares that have 1,000 per cent potential. A lot of writers, and I include myself here, believe we have seen another major market bottom lately after a bear market lasting four and a half years. Lots of stocks have already gone up 300 per cent and more.

If you have a stock that you want to buy because you want to make a 1,000 per cent profit, when do you sell?

The first thing you should do is come up with a plan. I have seen far too many investors buy a stock and pray. It goes to the moon, they don't sell, it collapses and they get forced out. That happens about

80 per cent of the time and if it fits your feet, wear it. That's why you are reading the book.

If you don't invest to make money, you are being foolish. The way to make money is to sell at a profit. If you refuse to sell at a profit, you won't make a profit. I keep repeating that because it's so important.

Let's take NovaGold for example. It went from $.09 in the spring of 2001 to $20. A reasonable plan to profit might be to sell 33 per cent of your shares when you have a double, sell another 33 per cent of the remainder when it doubles again, and a further 33 per cent every time it goes up another 100 per cent. That way you get most of your investment back in cash early on but keep benefiting if it goes up.

If you started with a 100,000-share position at $.09 for a $9,000 investment, and sold 33 per cent every time the stock doubled, by the time NovaGold hit $20 a share you would only have 1,990 shares left, worth $80,810, but you would have taken $157,366 off the table as profit.

So what do you do if you bought shares cheap and didn't sell on the way up? Well, while you are waiting for NovaGold to go to $40, it would go to $.46 as it did in 2008 and you would have gotten a margin call and lost it all. I know it happens because I know who it was who got the margin calls. And it wasn't me.

You can tell yourself that if you only had patience and faith, you could have had $2 million worth of stock that you paid only $9,000 for, but if you had patience and faith you would have ridden it creaming and cursing all the way back down to $.46, at which point you would give up and say you would never buy another penny dreadful.

Actually it makes a lot more sense to take money off the table when you can. Have a plan. Have any plan, but take some money off the table.

At any given time shares in a particular stock are either cheap or fairly priced or expensive. Those are all things you can figure out for yourself. If a stock has had a big run, it's no longer cheap. If everyone in the world loves it, it's probably expensive.

Nobody ever went broke taking a profit.

Chapter 8
The Next Big Thing

JAMES DINES has been inventing the next big thing for years. Doug Casey used to have the same ability but James Dines is the past master at creating or at least seeing in advance The Next Big Thing. He invents an industry; billions of investment dollars flow into the thinly-traded penny dreadfuls. The Next Big Thing collapses and becomes The Last Big Thing, leaving investors poorer and no wiser. Then he does it again.

If you happen to be a cynic — and I used to be but I just couldn't keep up — if you were a cynic you might suppose that he buys up a bunch of cheap shares before anyone gets it. Then he touts the industry to his massive e-mail list and his list of subscribers, then he cleans up. You can believe that if you want. It's probably so.

I don't want to take anything away from him. He is always one of the most interesting and informative speakers at any conference he attends. He also always has the hottest and tallest chicks at his booth pitching his subscription service and his books. Who can resist a tall hot chick?

James Dines does a wonderful job of marketing himself. There are others who try but can't quite measure up to his ability. So why shouldn't he make a little money?

But if you want to make money, you need to understand The Next Big Thing.

On the home page of his website, Dines elaborates on some of his better calls. On April 7 of 1997 he touted the upcoming Internet bubble and called himself the Original Internet Bug. That was a home run out of the park. He was an early adopter and the Internet shares rocketed up 8,246 per cent higher. And then they crashed. That was one of his better calls because the market was broad enough to absorb all the buying from his subscribers. That's not true of some of his later calls.

He was the original Uranium Bug starting in September of 2000. It went up 1,701 per cent before crashing in 2007. Then he moved on to become the Original Gold and Silver bug in 2001. Silver went up 977 per cent while gold lagged with a 558 per cent increase until they both crashed in 2011.

While Dines claimed to have been the Original Rare Earths Bug starting in 2009, actually if anyone deserves credit for foreseeing a boom in rare earth elements (REE) it would be John Kaiser of the Kaiser Report. Kaiser wrote one of the best pieces I have ever read about REE, and well before Dines "invented" REE.

In the past twenty years, we have seen an internet bubble bursting in 2000, then a real estate bubble bursting in 2007, gold and silver shooting higher before crashing in 2011, yet another stock market bubble popping in 2008, then the penny dreadfuls dropping as much as 99 per cent.

Do you see my point yet? The behavior of people runs in cycles. A guru discovers a new investment flavor of the week, money pours into the area, investors learn it's The Next Big Thing, more money flows in, shares double and triple and more. Then we have a crash and everything dies.

In the junior mining area, we had an early rush into Newfoundland in 2002 and 2003. Nobody found anything of merit. In 2009-2011 the same chumps poured money into every stock calling Colombia home. We had a molybdenum boom; we had a marijuana boom that lasted all of a few weeks. Lithium is in the midst of its boom right now. For a period, you could do no wrong if you invested in the Yukon. That was followed by a longer period where you could do no right if you invested in the Yukon.

What every investor needs to understand is that all markets are cyclical in nature. They go up and then they go down. And they go down twice as fast as they go up.

When I was young, stockbrokers pitched shares destined for "widows and orphans." They were touted as safe investments that threw off a dividend stream and they included municipal bonds, Polaroid, Kodak, AT&T, IT&T, Ford, GM, US Steel. Many of them are gone now.

The nature of business is that all things change. The hottest home computer, that every geek wanted to own in 1978-1980, was the Trash 80 or TRS-80 put out by Radio Shack. Now even Radio Shack is a shell of its former self and no one even remembers when they built computers.

For the longest time Microsoft dominated desktop computers. Then Steve Jobs came back to Apple and took the company from a three per cent market share to become the largest company in the world as measured by market capitalization. All things change. If you want to prosper, don't focus on finding the next big thing, focus on finding what will be The Last Big Thing and be the first to bail out.

There was a time you could marry your investments for life and pass them on to your kiddies. Those days are long gone.

Follow The Next Big Thing, invest in TNBT, but get out with a profit.

One of the most important issues with TNBT is the ability of that market to absorb investor capital. While the lithium, REE and moly manias rocketed share prices higher, the market simply didn't have room for companies with any reasonable story to invest in. Those manias didn't last long. I think the marijuana mania may have been the shortest I've ever seen, lasting little more than months. A few companies announced they were going to get into marijuana cultivation, their shares shot up, five hundred competitors jumped in with stories about how they were going to move from smoking marijuana into selling marijuana, and the market died.

How can you tell a market is about to collapse?

Look for a lot of stupidity. It's there if you look for it. In 1999 I was looking for companies in the gold mining area whose cash on hand exceeded their market capitalizations. Buying dollar bills at a discount always seems like a pretty good bet to me.

I found a tiny company that had a gold deposit in Colombia containing three million ounces. I started picking up shares. I think I was getting them at $.80 on the dollar. For all I knew, maybe someday people would want to own gold, and for all I knew, someone might want to invest in Colombia.

I went out on the Internet one day and found my shares had tripled in a couple of days. I looked into it to see just what it was that made a tiny gold company based in Colombia so desirable, other than having more cash in the bank than its market cap.

It was pretty simple. They had announced they were going into the Internet business. That's right, they were going to build computer furniture and sell it on the Internet, and that made them triple in days. That's pretty stupid. So I sold at a nice profit and bought the shares back after the Internet bubble crashed less than a year later.

When I read the story about inmates in a jail in Baltimore holding stock picking contests, I knew that bubble had just burst.

These are all things you can figure out for yourself. But you do need to understand the basics. You need to learn to think for yourself and to stop listening to the mass of disinformation pouring from every possible source.

James Dines' latest prediction calls for a gold bull market such as the world has never seen before. I don't disagree. It appears to have begun in late 2015. The initial jump out of the chocks for both gold and silver has been awesome. If we go into a booming gold market you need to remember that TNBT becomes TLBT at some point. If you want to profit, you have to sell. What goes up always goes down.

You are looking to identify the last possible fool to jump into a market. If you can find that fool, you have just picked the top in that market.

Likewise at market bottoms. You should be looking for the actions of governments because the dumbest bastards that ever drew breath run them. In 1999 Gordon Brown, Chancellor of the Exchequer in the UK, sold half of his country's gold reserves in a series of auctions. He managed to nail the very bottom of the gold market in August of 1999. Later they made him Prime Minister.

The Bank of Canada, run by Stephen Poloz, is giving Gordon Brown a run for his money in the "Worst Timing to Sell Gold" award. In February of 2016 Poloz sold off the last of Canada's gold reserves.

In an interesting press release, Poloz was quoted as justifying this action by the bank as a "long-standing policy of diversifying its portfolio by selling physical commodities (such as gold) and instead investing in financial assets that are easily tradable and that have deep markets of buyer and sellers."

For the "dumbest bastard running a country bigger than a postage stamp and as important as a loaf of bread," the gold sales timing award has to belong to President Nicolás Maduro of Venezuela. Venezuela was wise enough to repatriate its gold reserves in 2011 but faced with 720 per cent inflation and a 78 per cent probability of a credit default in 2016, Venezuela has been busy dumping its gold for months and will run out entirely soon. Their debt service costs for 2016 are estimated at $9.5 billion while their reserves are worth only $15.4 billion.

In Maduro's latest act of stupidity he has announced a week-long vacation for all workers, in order to conserve electricity. The government has subsidized the price of energy for years, to get votes. As a result, the poor use more electricity than is wise and the power grid has lacked for essential maintenance and upgrades.

I suppose he has a point. If you go on a permanent vacation, you will need less electricity to produce things. Of course the economy will then just stop, but that's next week, so who cares?

Chapter 9
Investing on News

MAINSTREAM MEDIA has brainwashed listeners for many years on a variety of subjects. One of the more interesting examples of this is the concept that news affects investments.

If you listen to or watch the six o'clock news, typically you will hear something like this: "The Dow dropped twenty points today because President Obama announced peace in the Middle East." Well, actually you may never hear that.

Or, "Gold was up twenty dollars today because the Dow dropped twenty points." What the media is trying to do is to convince you that news and investing are directly connected.

They are not. They aren't even indirectly connected for most of the time.

Markets are the products of thousands and sometimes millions of investment decisions made for a variety of reasons. No one sits by a computer waiting to buy gold depending on what the Dow does.

The mainstream media needs to fill airspace and they manage to fill it with a lot of hot air.

Now don't for a minute think that I am suggesting that the Internet is the font of all truth. The Internet is probably 75 per cent pure fiction and nonsense. But that's a far better record than that of the mainstream media, where close to 100 per cent of what they publish is rubbish or disinformation.

Even on days where we have been conditioned to believe that, say, Fed action will raise interest rates, will make gold go down and the dollar go up, many times if there is any reaction at all, it's the opposite of what conventional thinking would have you believe.

Markets move based on supply and demand as well as psychology. When left to their own devices, markets do a good job of discounting the future in the endless search for the correct price.

But the idea that the Dow or gold or any other financial instrument is waiting for news to react to is fatally flawed. It just isn't so.

Chapter 10
Does Manipulation Really Matter?

MY FIRST INVESTMENT in the stock market was in May of 1970. I had been buying gold as early as 1969 but as sort of an informal insurance policy, not for profit. While I was in Vietnam with the Marines I looked around at the cost and thought that owning something real might just be a good idea.

In any case, I bought my first financial investment in May of 1970. Stockbrokers had a lot of time for clients back then. Commissions were fixed and quite high. If you were a broker with a solid book of clients you made a lot of money. I can't prove it but I seem to recall there were a lot of brokers who actually understood markets.

Intuitively they understood, because they could see it on a daily basis, that all financial markets are manipulated. And they are manipulated all of the time.

Nobody talked about manipulation as if it was some evil to be fought to the death. Brokers and clients understood that everyone was trying to move the market, including themselves. Of course markets are manipulated. So?

Along came a guy who needed to make money on the web, since he had lost all his investment in a poorly-timed copper bet. Another guru tells him to set up a subscription website along with a non-profit website touting some evil in the financial arena.

So overnight the issue of "manipulation as the greatest evil in affairs financial" was created. Our guru of the day pronounced that he knew that it was both true and evil because he had overheard a conversation in Central Park, and this guy said that Long Term Capital Management went broke because they had a giant gold short position.

I am the only person who has ever even mentioned it, but if basing investment decisions on what some fool overheard in Central Park isn't stupid enough for you, failing to do your math when given a simple financial equation is.

When LTCM went broke in 1998, gold was the cheapest it had been since 1978. Now since LTCM was founded only in 1994, they couldn't possibly have shorted gold since 1978, but let's pretend they either did so or took over someone else's position.

If you own a gold short position and the price of gold goes down, you make money. So if gold in 1998 was at the lowest price that it had been since 1978, by definition you had a winning position. A company goes belly up when it makes unprofitable investments, not when it makes profitable investments.

Notwithstanding the fact that LTCM officials even gave sworn testimony that they had never traded gold in any form, long, short, physical, paper, options, futures, our guru has maintained for eighteen years that they were short, and that somehow put them into bankruptcy. Even if basic and simple math proves that what he claims simply could not possibly be true.

Don't you just hate it when facts prove your fantasies false?

The instant acceptance of the theory of manipulation as a giant evil to be fought at every level convinced another self-proclaimed guru, this time in silver, to make the incredible claim that it wasn't gold that was the most manipulated financial market in history, it was actually silver that was the more manipulated.

And silver was so rare that you should "never, never, never, ever sell silver." In fact it was so manipulated that by December of 2001 the world was going to run out of above-ground silver.

At the time, our hapless guru claimed that the world was down to one billion ounces of silver above ground, which meant that 98 per cent of all the silver ever mined had simply vanished into thin air. Silver got down to about $4 an ounce in November of 2001, the lowest in real terms that it had been in history.

December came and went and anyone needing silver could buy all they wanted. If there was a shortage it was a shortage known to only one person.

Guys running subscription websites either have to have some special knowledge that makes paying them to share it with you worth your while, or they have to cater to your fantasies, no matter how far-fetched. Since these self-proclaimed gurus hate having their bubbles pierced, they are more than willing to put words in the mouths of those pointing out the fantasy.

So I'll put it in writing one more time, so no one is confused. All financial markets are manipulated all of the time, perhaps legally, perhaps not. It is utter rubbish to claim that gold is manipulated or silver is manipulated without at least casually mentioning that so are all other financial markets.

We know the government believes it has the right to manipulate interest rates, and currencies, and maybe the stock market or any other market. So what? We still invest because we know that no matter what governments do, markets go up and markets go down.

Let's for argument's sake accept that the price of gold is being held down and that this is evil. How do you invest? Do you buy gold in the knowledge that the suppression is bound to fail, or do you sell gold because you realize that governments are all-powerful?

Actually you don't do either because it doesn't matter if gold is suppressed or not, nor that it's evil if it is suppressed. A belief that gold is manipulated is interesting but it's noise, not signal.

My objection to the manipulation and conspiracy crowd isn't because I care if they are right or not. I know that they are wrong. But there are a lot of wrong things in the world that don't bother me in the slightest because there is nothing I can do about them.

My objection is that their followers are losing hundreds of millions or billions of dollars by chasing their tails. If you bought into the gold manipulation theory in August of 1999 and were buying gold knowing the suppression was bound to fail, by September of 2011 you were sitting on a 600 per cent profit. But rather than suggest that their followers consider the effects of a gold correction, they continued playing that one-string banjo, screeching "buy" even after a wonderful opportunity to take a profit.

Gold's movement from $252 an ounce to $1,923 was cast iron proof it wasn't being suppressed. I have charts showing that as of September 2011 gold had gone up more since 1970 than any other metal. It wasn't a laggard, it was leading higher.

Likewise with silver moving from $4 in late November of 2001 to almost $50 in April of 2011, it was way overdue for a correction. If it was being manipulated, it was being manipulated higher, not lower.

Chapter 11
Buzz Words that Illuminate

WORDS HAVE MEANING. Or at least they should. Part of our communication with each other is based on accepting the meaning of certain words that we use in common. When you are a child you might make up words but you soon realize that if others don't know what you mean, the words are worthless.

I followed the wars in Afghanistan and Iraq closely because they were so foolish. I've already had a lot of experience with a really stupid war. When it comes to war, I've been there and have some idea of how wars work as a result.

Back in 2003 when we were engaged in yet another war with Iraq, I read reports about a 15,000-pound "daisy cutter" bomb. Since I was familiar with both the 15,000-pound bomb dropped out of a C-130 and the Daisy Cutter fuse, I read the article carefully so I could be sure I understood just what it said.

When we were dropping bombs to create a helicopter landing zone in Vietnam, typically we used 500 and 750-pound bombs with Daisy Cutter fuses. The fuse was like a long tube, 36 inches long, that exploded when its nose hit the ground three feet ahead of the bomb. As a result, all of the power of the bomb went sideways and chopped down all of the jungle, like cutting daisies. A Daisy Cutter was a fuse, not a bomb.

But the ignorance of the press is such that once they hear a buzzword, they all want to parrot it. So when the military announced that they had dropped a 15,000-pound bomb with a Daisy Cutter fuse, the media somehow misunderstood a Daisy Cutter to be a big bomb. You immediately knew from their misuse of a buzzword that they didn't know what they were talking about. In that instance, the use of the buzzword illuminated the ignorance of the writer rather than the knowledge of the reader.

Likewise, when in 2007 President Bush announced the assignment of an additional 20,000 troops to Iraq in response to increased activity on the part of the insurgents, he called it a "surge."

There was one slight technical problem with his use of the word "surge" in a military context. There is no such principle. You could pick up a thousand books about the military, in any language, and never see the word used. Because there was no such concept, until Bush needed a buzzword to describe what was nothing more than reinforcement. When the press all started writing about the surge, no one bothered pointing out that it wasn't a military term and really didn't mean much of anything. Bush and the press that parroted him were doing nothing more than advertising their ignorance.

In my experience no more than 20 per cent of the people who write about financial matters actually understand what they are talking about. I don't mean people who totally agree with me as that isn't a requirement, but people who are honest and who understand their field of endeavor. Only rarely do any of the 20 per cent appear on television, as the mainstream media hates people who know their jobs and tell the truth as they see it. Television is entertainment, not enlightenment. Financial reporting on the boob tube is about as real as wrestling.

I'd guess half the people writing or selling subscriptions about financial matters are outright frauds. They make stuff up and do everything in their power to convince you that the way to your fortune is to give them money. In return they will feed all your fantasies right back to you on demand.

The remaining 30 per cent are parrots. All they do is parrot what they hear. They can parrot the good guys or the frauds, they don't seem to care, but they don't have an original thought or concept in their little pea brains. In all cases, the parrots are trend followers, not leaders, and they love to use buzzwords to gain the credibility in which they otherwise would be lacking.

There are certain words used in finance which, when you hear them, tell you at once about the qualifications of the person using them. In most cases, the words were simply made up as part of one fraud or another.

One of my long time favorites was the concept of

a "gold derivatives time bomb." Bill Murphy of Gata invented this phrase over seventeen years ago. He made it up as part of a scheme to get people to subscribe to his subscription website. The central theme of the Gold Derivatives Time Bomb was that there was so much gold sold short that couldn't possibly be covered that one day soon, hopefully, the time bomb would go off and gold would be up hundreds of dollars in a day.

Now, having been in the military and having some basic understanding of bombs, it seems pretty obvious at least to me that a time bomb had to detonate within some reasonable period of time, else it wasn't a time bomb and perhaps not a bomb at all.

Millions of dollars were invested in gold by punters who were secure in the knowledge that their guru had proclaimed a time bomb was going to go off at any time that would make them richer overnight.

Well, seventeen years later I can assure you with the greatest of confidence that the Murphy made it up to get subscribers. There was no Gold Derivatives Time Bomb of any sort. Anyone using the phrase wasn't trying to illuminate the state of the gold market; he was either a parrot or part of the original fraud.

What happened was that one person began to use it and all of a sudden all of the sheep started to repeat a concept they had heard about but had not investigated. It meant they had no clue as to what they were mumbling about.

Shortly after the Gold Derivatives Time Bomb had passed its expiration date, Murphy began to spout rubbish about how the "clearing" price for gold was $600 an ounce. Gold had been as low as $252 in August of 1999, and after a short spurt higher to about $330 settled between about $350 and $255 for the next three years.

Certainly someone suggesting that gold might go to $600 might well be correct. Stranger things had happened. But Murphy acted as if he were an expert with all sorts of inside contacts. Everyone knows that experts use a lot of buzzwords so he began to mumble about the "market clearing price for gold."

It meant something like the correct price for gold was $600 an ounce. At $600 an ounce all the longs would cover, all the shorts would cover and gold would remain at $600, presumably forever. Now I had been a commodity broker for a short period in 1984 and I had studied economics and frankly I had never heard the term before. I don't think anyone else had either, for he made it up all by himself.

But once Murphy began to talk about the Market Clearing Price for Gold it was on everyone's tongue. Certainly it had to mean something. Since his mantra or the tune on his single-string banjo for years was that because of the manipulation and suppression of gold, gold was going to go to the moon any day now, I asked him how that fit in with his "clearing price" of $600.

What would happen, say, if gold shot up to $650? Would he then be telling his choir to sell their stash?

For some reason he never answered me. Gold hit $600 an ounce in 2006 and never looked back. The "clearing price" concept was both popular and perfectly accurate until it wasn't.

I think the first time I heard about a "commercial signal failure" was in late 2004. It was the same guy who made up the Gold Derivatives Time Bomb and the Market Clearing Price, Bill Murphy. As long as I have been aware of his site, he has pretended to be some kind of commodities insider. That was always interesting to me because it was clear he was telling people what they wanted to hear in order to get subscribers and was simply winging it. The closest he came to being an important insider was getting thrown out of the commodities business permanently and receiving the second-biggest fine in CFTC history. Some insider.

In late 2004 Murphy started talking about a "commercial signal failure." It had something to do with the shorts in gold being overwhelmed and gold being about to explode. I wrote to him in December of 2004 and suggested that his timing was once again perfect, since I had realized that every time he said the shorts were on the run, it marked a market top. He claimed he knew gold was going to the moon. Maybe so, but his first call in 2004 marked a top.

The next time I saw the buzzword used again was

in early March of 2008. The actual gold and silver top was about March 17, and so again, his screeching about a Commercial Signal Failure marked more of a top than a bottom.

If you hear someone talking about a Commercial Signal Failure you may want to ask them just where they learned about it, because it's not mentioned in any book about futures trading. Someone made it up and everyone else using it is a parrot or worse.

From about 2005 until well into the 2008 election cycle, hundreds of people were talking about the "North American Union". It was some kind of secret plan hatched by the governments of Mexico, the US and Canada to amalgamate the three countries into a union similar to the EU.

All of the people writing about it seemed to have inside information and they all just knew it was a done deal. Certainly with so many people writing and talking about it, it just had to be true. Proof positive came when people claimed to have seen the new currency for the union, the Amero.

There was no North American Union. There was no Amero. They either made it up or parroted those who did make it up. It was fiction.

With commodities, some markets are giant and some are tiny. We have had futures contracts for eggs, for potatoes, and for markets as small as that of mercury. Futures markets have been around in one form or another for 6,000 years.

The concept is simple. Producers need a stable source of their raw materials and consumers need a stable source of the finished products. Since producers may not have the product just when consumers need them, the use of futures contracts ensures that a third group, that of speculators, provides the necessary liquidity. Speculators make their money by correctly predicting future prices.

It's a true zero sum game. For every active contract, there is one buyer and one seller. Neither the buyer nor the seller is required to own the product or to take delivery; they can buy or sell a futures contract merely by putting up the minimum margin.

Everyone puts up either the product or the margin. That's fixed and absolute.

Since a market can be big or small, it's possible in theory that one big player could buy up all of a commodity and force the price much higher. So with all futures markets, the exchanges allow for cash delivery. If you bought a contract of gold for $1,150 and it went to $1,550 and there wasn't any gold, you would be paid in cash.

That brings up our first buzzword fantasy. If you ever hear that an exchange is on the verge of a default due to a lack of product, you know you are listening to someone trying to defraud you. The exchange provides for cash settlement. There cannot be a default under any circumstances. Period. It's not possible.

So when you hear anyone saying that "The

Comex is on the verge of a gold default" or a silver default, you know you are listening to either a con man, someone totally ignorant of how commodity markets work, or a parrot.

Likewise with the concept of a "naked short." Those tiny but extremely vocal groups espousing a theory of gold and silver having been suppressed are actually pretty quiet about how it could be done. On occasion they will throw out the idea that some nefarious body is selling gold or silver without the ability or intent to deliver so they are "naked shorts."

Unfortunately anyone using the term "naked short" is ignorant of how commodities really work. If you go back to how commodities function, neither buyer nor seller is committed to producing or accepting the product. There are producers, there are consumers, and there are speculators to provide liquidity.

If you sell something in the futures markets, there is no legal or moral or even logical reason for you to own it. You can sell anything short just by putting up the required margin. While there are limits to how many contracts you can sell, obviously there are ways to get around that. But since it's a zero sum market, there have to be buyers for all of the contracts you want to sell short.

If there was really such a thing as a "naked short", and the scammers have pretty much defined that as someone without the ability to deliver, wouldn't there logically be a "naked long" who has no intention of taking, or ability to take and pay for, full delivery? You will hear the term "naked short" because people are trying to get money from you but you will never hear them talk about a "naked long." But you couldn't possibly have one without the other.

Perhaps the most outrageous use of a buzzword to con readers came in 2009, when two subscription websites began talking about the discovery of gold-plated tungsten bars in Hong Kong being passed off as gold. One site claimed to have contacts who were saying that someone in Hong Kong had discovered there were between 5,600 and 5,700 gold-plated 400-ounce tungsten bars. What's more, according to this site, between 1.3 and 1.5 million tungsten bars had been made in the US around 1994, and 640,000 of the tungsten blanks were gold-plated and shipped to Fort Knox.

Good scammers understand that you need to sound as if you know what you are talking about so they will bury the reader or listener in meaningless factoids.

But to figure out if the story is true, you need to think. And today that's a rare skill.

All "good delivery" gold bars are tracked. No one is shipping bars worth $500,000 apiece without strict controls. You cannot walk into any establishment in the world and simply sell a 400-ounce bar without a lot of proof of who you are and where the gold came from. And the first thing they do is melt the bar and assay it again with the correct weight and purity.

So if there were any fake 400-ounce gold bars out there, they would show up quickly. It's been over six years since the discovery of the "fake story" and not a single 400-ounce gold-plated tungsten bar has shown up anywhere in the world.

But would it even be possible to do such a thing? Could you take a tungsten bar and coat it with gold and convince someone to buy it?

It's true that tungsten has a very similar specific gravity to gold. The SG of gold is 19.32 times that of water. Tungsten is a similar 19.22. The two are close enough in specific gravity that similar coins or bars made of each metal would be very close in size.

But could you fool those you need to fool? Actually, no. It wouldn't make any sense to make 400-ounce bars. You can go to Alibaba today and look up gold-plated tungsten. They have a wide variety of fake one ounce coins and bars. Why would someone attempt faking a 400-ounce bar when you can buy all the one-ounce tungsten fakes you want for a couple of bucks apiece on Alibaba? In a form that people can buy and sell and which you might get away with. You would never in a million years get away with selling a 400-ounce bar of tungsten.

And the two websites trying to convince people that they had some kind of inside special knowledge ignored some basics. Tungsten is very hard and takes a lot of heat to melt. In theory you could produce the 1.3 million bars the original instigator of this rumor claimed. They would have to be cast and milled and every one of them would be identical to the others.

While gold coins are not serialized, bars all have serial numbers, with the exception of the old 10-tola bars. If you cast and milled the big bars with serial numbers they literally would be too perfect. You see, all 400-ounce bars are cast in a mold and the serial number is hand stamped onto the bar. And good delivery bars may weigh anywhere between 350 and 430 ounces. Literally there is no such thing as an exact 400-ounce bar, there are only bars around 400 ounces. Not only the weight but the purity of the gold would vary as well. So while coins are all identical, 400-ounce bars all differ in size, weight, purity and markings.

So our con men are not only making up nonsense about fake gold bars in the 400-ounce range, they are ignoring the real danger that a lot of the one-ounce coins or bars are in fact gold-plated. The guys making stuff up to convince people to pay them for a subscription are ignoring a real problem and fabricating an imaginary problem.

Most coin dealers and people buying and selling pure gold learn to recognize the difference between fake coins and real coins. While the surface of a tungsten coin may test pure, the act of plating the tungsten core softens the lettering and image on the coin. A dealer can look at a fake and know.

The danger of the gold-plated tungsten bars isn't that of being conned by someone trying to score by selling you one, it's being conned by the guy making up the story to convince you he has special inside information. He doesn't. He made it all up to get subscribers.

Chapter 12
This Time It's Different

WHEN BUBBLES BURST, as they always do, you will hear one claim just as the bubble meets the needle: "This time it's different." When you hear those words, and you always will, run, don't walk to the nearest exit.

As I think I have showed in example after example, nobody knows anything. All you are ever hearing is someone's opinion. But more and more people get caught up in each crisis. The herd instinct kicks in, and since everyone else is involved, why shouldn't I be?

Every bubble ends in tears. The old measures of valuation really do apply still and all disasters are the mirror image of each other.

The most dangerous words in investing are, "This time it's different."

Chapter 13
If A = B and B = C, Does A = C?

A CENTURY AGO, when I was in high school, one of my teachers wanted to teach us the basics of logic. The teacher began with a simple equation: if A = B and B = C, does A = C? Of course the majority of the class picked the most obvious answer.

But what happens when the apparent answer is not the correct answer? What if the obvious is dead wrong?

Here is the proof. If an airplane is transportation and a train is transportation, is an airplane the same as a train? Now the correct answer is both apparent and obvious. No. A train and an airplane are both transportation but they are not the same.

As investors, why is this important for us to know? Because there is far more noise in the investment community than signal.

For example, if you knew that silver had climbed from $4.01 an ounce in November of 2001 to $49 and change in April of 2011, then by using nothing but your own common sense you could reasonably conclude that silver was cheap in 2001 relative to silver in 2011. And that it was expensive in 2011 relative to what it had been in 2001.

You didn't need to know anything else in order to make an intelligent decision. If you did nothing more than buy silver when it was cheap and sell it when it got expensive, you could have made a lot of money; 1,140 per cent, in fact. Nobody did, of course, because they were too busy listening to the experts.

All of the gurus were mumbling about how high silver was going to go. Silver was somehow moving from weak hands into strong hands.

The loudest voice in silver had been claiming since at least 2001 that silver would go up ten or twenty-fold if the US ever got into another war, since it was the most valuable war material. The US had half a dozen wars to choose from so silver had to take off and go even higher.

There was even a group that managed to convince people that while silver was going from $4 to $50 it was being suppressed. Now you have to wonder at the gullibility of some people. How many people are actually dumb enough to watch a commodity enter into one of the greatest bull markets in history and still maintain that it is being suppressed?

On the other hand, an ordinary person of average intelligence could access the bullish consensus data on silver at the very top of the market on January 21, 1980 and learn that it was 94 per cent. If all you knew was that the bullish consensus is always at its highest at market tops and at its lowest at market bottoms, you could have made a very profitable decision in late April of 2011. All you had to do was to understand the basics of investing.

If the bullish consensus was 94 per cent at the very top of the silver market in 1980, and if the bullish consensus was 96 per cent in April of 2011 (which it was), then no matter what the gurus or experts said, we were probably at a top. Everyone could have arrived at that conclusion; they didn't need to listen to anyone else. Yes, they would need access to information. You would have to be able to find out the price of silver, and its price history. And you would need to follow one of the services tracking bullish consensus. But all that information is at your fingertips now because of the Internet.

You would need to know the basics of investing because none of the experts or gurus wants you to think. They want your money, and the only way to do that is to keep you ignorant. So they take your money and tell you what you want to hear. A lack of money is the root of all evil.

It's a very successful business plan; politicians have been using it for centuries. If you tell people what they want to hear, they will vote for you. That's just as true in investing as it is in the voting booth.

I can give you another perfect example where the use of simple, basic logic can help you make intelligent investing decisions instead of following the rest of the lemmings over the cliff. Recently Deutsche Bank admitted it had been manipulating the gold fix. This manipulation was accomplished in the same way that high-frequency traders clip cents off every stock trade;

117

the bank was front running its customers.

The various banks running the gold fix have to know how supply and demand meet at a specific point in time, in order to determine what the fix should be. So if demand was high, the participants in the fix would set the price just slightly higher than supply and demand would dictate.

If demand was low, they set the price slightly lower than it should have been. Since all markets move both up and down to determine the "right" price, their manipulation was both up and down, and didn't last for long before supply and demand resumed getting the price right.

If Deutsche Bank manipulated the gold fix, and if long-term price suppression is manipulation, is manipulation equal to suppression? No, of course not. Because while suppression is always manipulation, manipulation isn't always suppression.

So when you read a financial guru telling you how Deutsche Bank admitting that it manipulated the fix really means that gold was suppressed all the way from $252 an ounce to $1,923, you can logically determine if you really want to be giving them your hard-earned money. Manipulation isn't necessarily suppression, and any commodity that goes from $252 to $1,923 isn't being suppressed.

The Next Big Thing in investing is probably going to be commodities. All commodities had a peak in 2011, not only silver and gold. They have suffered a terrible and costly bear market, not only silver and gold. They *all* hit bottom late in 2015 and early in 2016. It's just as true of sugar and coffee as it is of gold and silver. And while a lot of people still want to mumble about how gold is being suppressed, it is factual to say that platinum and oil went down a lot more. Nobody is claiming they were suppressed. You can use your common sense in investing. It is not only a good idea, it is probably mandatory.

On the next page is a ten-year chart of the Bloomberg Commodity index, BCOM. It shows a high in mid-2011 in all commodities and a low in early 2016. That's for all commodities, not just oil, gold and silver.

When the train finally arrives at the station loaded with bags of money just for you, you don't want to be at the airport.

Books on Amazon are now dynamic. I can add a chapter to *Nobody Knows Anything* in a day. If readers think I have missed something and have suggestions as to something I should add, please send me an email.

All commodities, including gold and silver, are going to go up a lot. There will be a time when they get expensive. A time will come to sell both gold and silver before they become The Last Big Thing.

Chapter 14
Tools I Use

WHILE I HAVE ATTEMPTED to give readers some of what I think are the most important basics of investing, obviously you have to use other tools to get information.

I'm going to give readers a list of some of the sites I use to find information. I have no relationship with them whereby I get paid, so it doesn't matter to me financially if you sign up with them or not. These are just people I know and like – like a lot, in some cases.

1. The best source of free information on the web for current metals prices is Kitco.com. Everyone uses them. We link to their site for our data.

2. The single best site for paid charts and data of anything metals-related has to be Nick Laird of goldchartsrus.com. He charges $200 for a year's subscription. If you don't know if you need his service or not, he will give you a three-week trial for $10. If you want to trade the gold/silver ratio or platinum/gold spread, his site is invaluable. He can be reached at nick@goldchartsrus.com

3. In my view the single best writer on the web writing about things financial would be Grant

Williams of Things That Make You Go Hmmm... Ttmygh.com. He charges $295 for a one-year subscription. I've always felt the best all round writer of the last 50 years was Richard Russell, but he left us. Grant is just as good. He doesn't give specific investment advice, he just sends out 22 issues a year of interesting stuff. Send him an email at info@ttmygh.com and request a trial subscription. It's well worth it. I just don't know how he writes so much, so well. I couldn't do it.

4.   Bob Hoye of Institutional Advisors has one of the finest and most accurate subscription services on the web at institutionaladvisors.com. The service is aimed at high net worth individuals and portfolio managers. He is very good. For a free 30-day trial, email r.brian.ripley@gmail.com. The service is not cheap but if you want the best in anything, you have to pay for it. Except for me. I'm free.

5.   Here is another very valuable service for those who need a feel for the market and what is going on. RealVisionTV.com delivers 150 interviews a year with the greatest names in finance for $364 (less than a dollar a day). They offer a free one-week trial.

6. If you want to really make money, you need to understand and use the bullish consensus numbers. There are two services offering bullish consensus. I use consensus-inc.com. They provide weekly readings on 32 commodity markets. Yearly service is $312 and they do offer a one-week free trial. Market Vane offers a similar service that costs $25 a month for daily updates and $45 a month for weekly updates. They are at MarketVane.net. If you can pick one top or bottom in any market using nothing but bullish consensus, you have more than paid for ten years of either or both of these services.

7. I'm coming around to the opinion that all investors, including myself, tend to overthink investment decisions. I've been watching James Flanagan of Gann Global Financial for years. He has been nailing both market tops and bottoms for years. His work showed me that while the vast majority of commentators on the metals tend to zoom in and micro analyze every twist and turn in gold and silver, actually all the metals have been doing since 2011 is tracking all the other commodities. You didn't have to worry about what was happening with gold, as sugar and coffee were doing exactly the same thing. GannGlobal.com is probably worth looking at closely. Gann offers a free trial and a variety of

different packages. I recommend him highly. He is not a gold or silver guy, he covers everything.

8. For up-to-the-minute quotes on Canadian and US stocks, you might try StockWatch.com or StockHouse.com. They both offer a lot of free information and have some paid services. I use StockWatch constantly and pay about $12 a month.

9. The superb Steve Saville runs The Speculative Investor. He provides two reports weekly covering the stock market, commodities, bonds, currencies and precious metals. He understands how and why the markets work as well or better than anyone I know. The site can be found at speculative-investor.com. When there is an issue of bad or poor information becoming commonly accepted, Steve does a wonderful job of explaining how and why a particular market functions as opposed to how the herd believes it functions. The site is makes the cost of $25 monthly or $240 a year seem pretty cheap.

10. We provide our readers on 321gold.com with a wide variety of opinions from both paid and free sites. I can't list every site or writer that I like and use, as I do this 8-10 hours a day and cover a lot of territory. We will post any reasonable opinion, no matter if we agree or not. There is a lot of

parroting on gold sites. You can see the same opinions posted again and again without a vestige of either logic or fact included. If it's not either factual or logical, we won't post it.

11. Tom McClellan puts out the McClellan Market Report at $195 a year and The Daily Edition at $600 a year. Like Bob Hoye, the research and timing is magnificent and well worth the price. There's a 14-day free trial offer for new subscribers at Mcoscillator.com. The market reports are published approximately monthly.

12. One of the finest minds and best writers can be found for free on our site, on Fridays. Adam Hamilton's site is called Zealllc.com. The service costs $119 yearly and is cheap at half the price. In April of 2011 he was one of the very few calling a top in silver. In December of 2015 he nailed the bottom in gold and silver. He is neither a guru nor an expert. He just calls them as he sees them, with great accuracy.

You are allowed to think for yourself. There are a lot of people who don't want you thinking for yourself. We think it's a great idea if you will think for yourself.

Made in United States
North Haven, CT
20 April 2022

18422439R00082